# PICKING
## *Up the*
# PIECES
## HANDBOOK

*Creating a Dynamic Soul-Care Ministry in Your Church*

Chuck Hannaford

LifeWay Press®
Nashville, Tennessee

# PICKING UP THE PIECES HANDBOOK
*Creating a Dynamic Soul-Care Ministry in Your Church*

© 2009 Chuck Hannaford, PhD

Published by Serendipity House Publishers
Nashville, Tennessee

IBSN: 978-1-5749-4344-3
Item Number: 005038470

To purchase additional copies of this resource or other studies:
ORDER ONLINE at *www.SerendipityHouse.com,* FAX 615-277-8081
WRITE Serendipity by LifeWay, One LifeWay Plaza, Nashville, TN 37234

1-800-458-2772
*www.SerendipityHouse.com*

Printed in the United States of America

# CONTENTS

# About the Author

## Chuck Hannaford, PhD

Dr. Chuck Hannaford is a licensed clinical psychologist with a private practice and is executive director of HeartLife Professional Soul-Care in Germantown, Tennessee. He has been counseling individuals, couples, and families for 28 years. He earned his doctorate from the University of North Texas and served his internship in clinical psychology at the University of Tennessee, Medical School, Division of Psychiatry, and Department of Clinical Psychology. After completion of his internship year, Dr. Hannaford cofounded Germantown Psychological, which he left in 1999 in order to devote himself fully to consult with churches and pastors to teach, train, and counsel from a Christian psychology perspective. He has served as clinical director of adolescent and adult treatment programs at various hospitals and outpatient settings. In the past he served as the president and chief executive officer of Germantown Psychological Associates, P.C., director of professional relations for the Rapha Christ Centered Treatment Program in Memphis, consultant to Bellevue Baptist Church, Germantown Baptist Church, and executive director for Christian Wellness Concepts.

Dr. Hannaford has published articles in professional journals on the relationship between physical and spiritual well-being and emotional health. He coauthored *HealthWay*, a strategic discipleship intervention for physical, emotional, and spiritual health. He has been a guest on nationally syndicated Christian radio shows discussing biblically based counseling and the family.

In addition to his current practice, Dr. Hannaford has been a consultant to LifeWay Christian Resources, churches, and pastors throughout the country. He is clinical professor of biblical counseling at The Southern Baptist Theological Seminary. Hannaford and his wife Laura are members of Germantown Baptist Church in Germantown, Tennessee.

# DEDICATION

*I dedicate this book to the countless souls who have shared their stories with me over the years. Thank you for trusting me with your pain and allowing me to be part of your journey.*

# ACKNOWLEDGMENTS

I heard somewhere that no one has an original thought, and in my case that is certainly true. These concepts belong first and foremost to our Lord Jesus Christ, the cure for our souls.

I express my deep love and appreciation to my best friend and wife, Laura. Your advice, love, and patience inspire me. Thank you for allowing me the time to write this. I am grateful to my son Chad who has challenged me to look into my heart and become a better father.

I owe much to many friends and colleagues, and I will not be able to name them all. Among them are those whose friendship and direction have been a source of support and helped shaped my thinking on soul care: Eric Johnson, Josh Creason, Tony Rose, Russell Moore, Danny Akin, Barney Self, Rob Mullins, Craig Parker, Jay Johnston, Bob Sorrell, David Powlison, Ed Welch, Mark Castellaw, Troy Jens, and Rick Sayger. Your love, support, and inspiration will never be forgotten. I must not forget my "family" at HeartLife Professional Soul-Care (Chip Pillow, Steve Riser, Brenda Gilman, Mary Margaret Johnson, and Erin Marie Cox); you keep me sharp. Thank you for catching the vision for our ministry. Finally, thanks to Germantown Baptist Church and the board of directors of HeartLife Professional Soul-Care: David Sayle, Beth Reed, Eric Arthur, Tom Savage, and Joe Kelley. You have made the vision of professional soul care a reality.

I acknowledge my deep love and gratitude to my spiritual father and former pastor, Adrian Rogers. His guidance and leadership challenged my secular training in the early years. I miss him greatly.

Thanks go to The Southern Baptist Theological Seminary and my students for allowing me to teach and refine this model of soul care. Students, thank you for teaching me.

I truly appreciate the team at LifeWay who made this book a reality: Ron Keck provided leadership, Chris Johnson managed the project through to completion, Darin Clark developed a great design direction, and Judi Hayes contributed strong editorial efforts to deliver a much-needed resource for churches. Finally, many thanks to Ben Colter who came alongside me, taking my words and making them better.

# INTRODUCTION

## TRANSFORMING PEOPLE, TRANSFORMING CHURCHES

*Excitement, happiness, adventure, love, laughter, freedom, beauty,* and *hope*—these words describe the kind of life we all long to experience. From the beginning we were created to live with passion and purpose, but we live in a sabotaged and fallen world in which suffering is the norm rather than the exception. When life is suddenly disrupted by loss, suffering, betrayal, or addictions, everything changes. Sometimes life is hard, and our pain feels unbearable.

But how do we manage the pain and suffering or escape the feelings of loss and emptiness that sometimes haunt us in the middle of the night? No one likes dealing with the hard stuff of life. Our God-given desires to find meaning, significance, belonging, adventure, and relational intimacy often send us searching in the wrong places for what we lack, trying to escape, numbing out, or spiraling into disillusionment and despair.

## ENGAGING THE MESSY REALITY

Christ followers are not immune to the tragedies of life or the evil attacks of the enemy. Jesus warned His followers and encouraged them in this way: "I have told you these things so that in Me you may have peace. You will have suffering in this world. Be courageous! I have conquered the world" (John 16:33). Peter gives this sober warning: "Your adversary the Devil is prowling around like a roaring lion, looking for anyone he can devour" (1 Pet. 5:8).

> We have no right to think that the type of relationships
> we have with others should be any different from those
> the Lord Himself had.
>
> —OSWALD CHAMBERS.

There has never been a time when we could separate and protect ourselves from the darkness and messiness of this world, so why do we pretend that we can? Our churches face new and daunting challenges in the 21st century. Now more than ever our congregations are filled with hurting people whose problems cannot be answered by pat churchy phrases or the empty promises of a secular therapeutic culture. Divorce, marital infidelity, the dissolution of the family, addictions, suffering, depression, and anxiety in the Christian community can no longer be ignored.

In the 1999 blockbuster movie *The Matrix*, the lead character Neo is given the choice to continue in an artificial world of disengaged peace or to engage reality with a band of brothers and sisters. Morpheus explains to Neo, "You take the blue pill—the story ends, you wake up in your bed and believe whatever you want to believe. You take the red pill—you stay in Wonderland and I show you how deep the rabbit-hole goes." Simply because you're reading this book, I know the blue pill is not working for you any more. You may, like Neo, have no idea how deep the rabbit hole of reality goes in the lives of hurting people, but you've had enough of living in an artificial world. You're ready to join Jesus in the real world of spiritual warfare, broken lives, shattered dreams, and redemption.

## Joining Jesus in His Mission to Set Captives Free!

> *Christ has liberated us into freedom. Therefore stand firm*
> *and don't submit again to a yoke of slavery.*
> —Galatians 5:1

Jesus sums up His ministry in Luke 4:18-19: "The Spirit of the Lord is on Me, because He has anointed Me to preach good news to the poor. He has sent Me to proclaim freedom to the captives and recovery of sight to the blind, to set free the oppressed, to proclaim the year of the Lord's favor." He came to set our hearts free and to redeem the hurt and shame embedded in our souls. He invites, even urges, us to join Him in freeing other captives and healing wounded hearts!

Biblical healing is not based on a form of Christian behavior modification (another way of trying to manage our sin). It's not giving Christ followers a scriptural text to memorize and telling them to call you in the morning. It's doing life together in such a way that our stories intermingle, our journeys intersect, our bondages break, our lives are redeemed, and our God is glorified. God strongly criticized the prophets and priests for applying superficial bandages to deep emotional and spiritual wounds in Jeremiah 6:14: "They have treated My people's brokenness superficially, claiming: Peace, peace, when there is no peace."

A soul-care ministry will not be vital and effective if it's unwilling to dive into the difficult areas of life with real people in a real world. Soul care will not work if it's event driven, highly programmed, sanitized, or focused on numbers. Effective and radical soul care is based first and foremost on a model of radical connection to Jesus and deep transformation. The foundation of effective and radical discipleship is relationship. Healing does not come with a formula; it's a lifelong process that's most effective in the context of redemptive community and vital relationships.

# Reenvisioning Church

> One life wholly devoted to God is of more value to God than one hundred lives simply awakened by His Spirit.
>
> —Oswald Chambers

What's the answer? How does a church grow in numbers, maturity, and effectiveness for the kingdom of God when the demand of damaged souls continues to increase? It's easy for pastors and church leaders to become overwhelmed by the sheer magnitude of the issues. Yet all of us—pastors, leaders, and church members—have responsibility in the care and cure of souls. We cannot transform our churches overnight. We must take people on a transformational journey, but it all begins with the choice to take the first step. Just remember, no matter how deep the hurt or the how dark the issues, God reaches deeper still and always brings light to His children.

> *This extraordinary knowledge is beyond me.*
> *It is lofty; I am unable to reach it.*
> *Where can I go to escape Your Spirit?*
> *Where can I flee from Your presence?*
> *If I go up to heaven, You are there;*
> *if I make my bed in Sheol, You are there.*
> *If I live at the eastern horizon*
> *or settle at the western limits,*
> *even there Your hand will lead me;*
> *Your right hand will hold on to me.*
> *If I say, "Surely the darkness will hide me,*
> *and the light around me will become night"—*
> *even the darkness is not dark to You.*
> *The night shines like the day;*
> *darkness and light are alike to You.*
>
> —Psalm 139:6-12

*Picking Up the Pieces Handbook* was designed to help you catch God's passion for those who are helpless, hurting, or in bondage—to help your church become a center for soul care. More than that, it gives you a practical guide to create a dynamic soul-care ministry that's not just one more program to add to your already busy church calendar. It's my prayer that this proven approach will radically transform your church and ministry regardless of the size of your congregation or community. It's time to stop doing church and focus on *being the church*!

Using this handbook, you'll be motivated and equipped to begin a soul-care ministry in your church. You'll discover how to develop and communicate vision, passion, and structure based on a simple but powerful model of prevention and intervention. Discover the solutions to accountability and liability issues, explore new ministry paradigms to promote health and healing, learn to recruit and equip effective leaders, and work toward recapturing the church's central role in soul care.

Let me briefly explain the structure of this book. Section 1 provides basic chapters about the essential nature of soul-care ministry in your church. Everyone in your church who is interested in soul care should read this section of the book. Section 2 is the training section. Everyone who wants to lead a Picking Up the Pieces small group needs to experience the training outlined here; these chapter provide both content and leadership ideas for the essential group training experience. Section 3 includes forms needed for Picking Up the Pieces leaders as well as forms for your church's soul-care ministry. Section 4 provides helpful resources for a soul-care ministry in your church beyond small-group experiences using Picking Up the Pieces resources. This information is critical for the protection of the church, establishing relationships with professionals, and creating structures for the development of a full-orbed soul-care ministry. Smaller churches may not have the resources to develop a full-orbed model, but the information provided in section 4 takes you through an indispensable thought process as you seek the best for your members. No matter the size of your church, I pray you will join us in our rich Christian heritage of soul care.

## BECOME A SOUL-CARE CENTER

- Vision and passion for the hurting

- An environment for transformation

- A structured process for accountability

- A dynamic, Spirit-guided process for healing

- Healing that leads to transformation

- Transformed people who enhance a church's mission

# THE
# SOUL-CARE CRISIS
## *in*
# OUR CHURCHES

> When Jesus Christ shed his blood on the cross, it was not
> the blood of a martyr; or the blood of one man for another;
> it was the life of God poured out to redeem the world.
>
> —OSWALD CHAMBERS

# CHAPTER 1

# PICKING UP
## *the Pieces* —
# A PROCESS,
## NOT A PROGRAM

The life I touch for good or ill will touch another life, and that in turn another, until who knows where the trembling stops or in what far place my touch will be felt.

—FREDERICK BUECHNER

This is the duty of our generation as we enter the twenty-first century—solidarity with the weak, the persecuted, the lonely, the sick, and those in despair. It is expressed by the desire to give a noble and humanizing meaning to a community in which all members will define themselves not by their own identity but by that of others.

—ELIE WIESEL

*The word of God is living and effective and sharper than any two-edged sword, penetrating as far as to divide soul, spirit, joints, and marrow; it is a judge of the ideas and thoughts of the heart.*
*—HEBREWS 4:12*

## LIVING OUR STORIES

Picking Up the Pieces is not about tacking yet another program onto an already burdened church. It's about fresh ways of looking at God, man, the larger redemptive story, pain, healing, community, and mystery—*the theology of our stories*. It's also about *a model and a process for doing church* in a more profound way that brings healing and empowers people to join Jesus in His mission to bind up the brokenhearted, set captives free, and replace beauty for ashes.

---

*Picking Up the Pieces*
1. *A fresh theology of our stories*
2. *A fresh model and process for doing church*

---

This handbook and the books in the Picking Up the Pieces series are about people, healing, and ministry. The series includes a number of topical group studies, leadership training models, and church resources. I want to explain why I chose to write the leadership handbook for this series. Other excellent products are available, but in my opinion no other resources have the cohesiveness, consistency, and heart focus offered by Picking Up the Pieces. I've been training leaders in topic-specific small groups for more than two decades, and I've reviewed my share of materials for these groups.

## FRACTURED LEADERSHIP CREATE ISSUES

I developed and led the first divorce recovery small group in my community. We found no suitable materials at the time, so over the first few years we developed some. During this time we also recognized that we needed other topic-specific groups dealing with death and loss, parenting, marriage, and other issues. We had to make it up as we went along. Soon other churches in our area began doing the same thing, and over time we began to witness the publication of materials for topic-specific small groups.

An interesting phenomenon was taking place. Churches were beginning to recognize the benefit of meeting people at specific points of need, but the results were mixed. Larger churches would put a member of the pastoral staff over a small-group ministry, and this pastor selected leaders for the groups. Some churches trained leaders while others did not. Smaller community churches, without the resources to develop this type of ministry, would send members to other churches in the area. Larger churches would add new groups each semester. Here is where it got interesting.

---

*Everything rises on focused leadership and falls on fractured leadership.*

---

The tail began wagging the dog. In other words, as the groups grew, the churches provided less and less oversight and continuity among them. Typically each leader would pick materials with which he or she was familiar; there were as many different resources as there were groups. This is when I first heard the phrase, *"Everything rises on focused leadership and falls on fractured leadership."*

In one megachurch the minister responsible for topic-specific small groups left his position with as many as 25 different groups meeting each Wednesday evening. The pastor realized there had been little accountability and leadership was fractured. Some groups were running 12 consecutive weeks and others 6. Some leaders had been trained, but many had not. Group participants freely moved among the groups, resulting in confusion. I was tasked with evaluating this ministry, and over the subsequent months we discovered several key things that allowed us to develop an effective, biblical small-group ministry.

Many of the same problems we found years ago still exist in discipleship and mentoring programs/ministries today. Here are a few of the key fractured leadership issues.

- Many of the group leaders operated independently, making referrals to professionals and giving advice that was clearly inconsistent with the church's doctrine or theological position. Some were essentially counseling without a license, creating liability issues for the church.
- Many of the resource materials were not consistent from a doctrinal or theological standpoint with the church or the denomination.
- Every semester attendance began to drop sharply after the eighth week. Most of the groups were running 12 weeks. At the end of 12 weeks, approximately 60 percent of attendees had dropped out.
- There was no selection process for group leaders; most of the group leaders had not been through any formal training, and they had little, if any, accountability.

Our solution at the time:

- We began to evaluate the small-group ministry and to meet with group leaders.
- We began formal training for group leaders.
- We began to research materials and training programs, electing in the end to develop our own.
- We determined it was best to keep all groups to a maximum of eight weeks.
- We educated the pastoral staff and Sunday School teachers and encouraged them to make people who were hurting aware of the topic-specific small-groups ministry.

- We developed topic-specific, small-group ministry to reach *in* to the congregation and *out* to the community.
- We began to see the unchurched come into the groups with our group leaders trained to minister to them and assist them in getting involved in a local church.

## FOCUSED LEADERSHIP AND APPROACH

Some leaders are beginning to recognize and support the development of the "relational ministry" component in churches, supported by professionals who work under ecclesiastical oversight. Strategic group and individual discipleship within the context of relationships should become a primary focus for strengthening people and helping free them from emotional and spiritual captivity. The Picking Up the Pieces series specifically targets healing groups led by trained laity and staff. Pastoral counseling, intervention, and guidance are still required but significantly diminished with this approach. Professional soul-care ministries actively engage with the church, providing support when the acuity of a situation is beyond minister/lay capability.

> *We need focused leadership and coherent materials.*

## PICKING UP THE PIECES APPROACH

Resource materials development is a difficult and expensive process. In consulting with churches about their development of topic-specific ministries, I've been troubled by a lack of continuity and consistency in the many resource materials. That is not the case with Picking Up the Pieces resources. Each Picking Up the Pieces study has been authored by one or more experts in the respective topics. Each author works closely with the editorial staff of Serendipity/LifeWay throughout product development to ensure doctrinal integrity, theological continuity, and consistent tone and message. This is critical since many group participants will begin in one group and find a need to go through one or more of the others. Most groups meet for an eight-week time frame to maximize attendance and participation.

The Picking Up the Pieces materials and group methodology provide essential training, structure, and consistency necessary to facilitate healing. Each resource provides focused leadership, consistent participant experiences, and a model that identifies future group leaders across the topics. All group leaders are given specific instructions each week. The approach is intentional and seamless while allowing for necessary freedoms within each venue.

> *We need transformation, not just information or sin management.*

As opposed to sprinkling secular psychologies into healing and recovery groups, Picking Up the Pieces resources have a solid focus on God's words in Scripture and on the presence and power of "Christ in you, the hope of glory" (Col. 1:27). The studies carefully balance individual responsibility with God's power to speak into and transform the heart.

> *God wanted to make known to those among the Gentiles the glorious wealth of this mystery, which is Christ in you, the hope of glory. We proclaim Him, warning and teaching everyone with all wisdom, so that we may present everyone mature in Christ.*
> —COLOSSIANS 1:27-28

With strong group dynamics, creative and experiential discipleship, and focus on matters of the heart, Picking Up the Pieces resources go way beyond instruction or merely managing sin to lead people on a transformational journey guided by the Holy Spirit. These resources identify underlying issues of the heart and then discuss and discover effective, realistic biblical solutions to meet hurting people at their point of need. Throughout this book you'll see repeated themes of community, authenticity, trust, transformation, and journey. Although Picking Up the Pieces resources provide a structure, each local church determines how the groups will interface with existing ministries.

We need to develop and equip laity for involvement in soul care and ministry. The goal of Picking Up the Pieces is to move people into a place of ministry to help others. Leadership should be chosen or approved by the pastoral staff or church leaders, and the training should ensure that all those chosen and trained are gifted and ready to lead a Picking Up the Pieces group. Picking Up the Pieces groups create a process, not another program. Every group leader should go through the training.

> *We need authentic spiritual communities that address issues before they become crises.*

CHAPTER 2

# WHAT
## *Is*
# SOUL
### CARE?

Here lies the tremendous mystery—that God should be all-powerful, yet refuse to coerce. He summons us to cooperation. We are honored in being given the opportunity to participate in his good deeds. Remember how He asked for help in performing His miracles: Fill the water pots, stretch out your hand, distribute the loaves.

—Elisabeth Elliot

*He came to Nazareth, where He had been brought up. As usual, He entered the synagogue on the Sabbath day and stood up to read. The scroll of the prophet Isaiah was given to Him, and unrolling the scroll, He found the place where it was written:*

> *The Spirit of the Lord is on Me,*
> *because He has anointed Me*
> *to preach good news to the poor.*
> *He has sent Me*
> *to proclaim freedom to the captives*
> *and recovery of sight to the blind,*
> *to set free the oppressed,*
> *to proclaim the year of the Lord's favor.*

*He then rolled up the scroll, gave it back to the attendant, and sat down. And the eyes of everyone in the synagogue were fixed on Him. He began by saying to them, "Today as you listen, this Scripture has been fulfilled."*

—Luke 4:16-21

Sarah and Tom have been married for almost 30 years. They have a secure, loving marriage and family. That foundation has helped them survive the past year, the most difficult year of their marriage. First, Sarah's mom got sick. Sarah had a difficult time juggling caring for her mom, meeting family needs, and doing her job. Eventually she took a leave of absence from her job. That created a financial strain on the family budget. Then her mom died. Exhausted and in grief, Sarah returned to work. But before the family budget had recovered, Tom's company cut a hundred jobs, and he was out of work and looking for a job in the worst economic downturn in decades. And if all of these crises were not enough, their son came home from college and announced that he was addicted to gambling, and his debts added to the family's financial troubles.

Sarah, Tom, and their kids survived this difficult year. Looking back, they say that the soul care provided by church members really made a difference. Here are some of the acts of caregiving they recall:

- When Sarah's mom got sick, women from her Sunday School class shared with her some of their experiences in caring for their mothers and told her they were always available to listen. Sarah found that she could safely share her exhaustion, sorrow, and even her anger. Sarah always felt love and understanding from these women.
- When Sarah was spending long hours with her mother, church members brought food to the family. When her mother died, people from the church took care of their house, made phone calls, enlisted substitutes for Sarah and Tom's responsibilities at church, and even stocked their refrigerator and freezer.
- After Sarah's mother died, she joined a grief group at church. As those people shared, bonds developed that have continued in friendship after the group ended.
- Church friends took Tom out for lunch and golf when he lost his job. They made sure he knew that he was a valuable and gifted friend. They kept him from feeling isolated and alone. They made contacts and helped him network. Eventually one of their tips led to a new job.
- Both Sarah and Tom recall moments in worship that touched them deeply during this time. The pastor was a source of ongoing support and encouragement.
- The young adult minister at the church helped Tom and Sarah's son secure counseling and get involved in a support group that helped him overcome his gambling addiction.

The problems Sarah and Tom and their son faced during one year's time are common to the crises families face every day. The ministries their church performed are business as usual in many churches. That's the nature of soul care. It's what Jesus taught. It's what the early church modeled, and it's being church at its best today. It's taking God's love to people in need.

Healing touches from God result in transformed people, and transformed people transform churches and communities. As Sarah and Tom's life began to return to a manageable pace, they wanted to provide soul care for others as they had received it. They have found a number of ways to do this. Both of them are now training to lead small groups of people who are hurting.

That's what this book is all about—soul care. It takes place in many churches every day. This book will explore the concept of soul care, look at the need for soul care as it is shaped in the world today, and help your church take its soul care to the next level. Those next-level steps may include providing small-group ministries facilitated by trained leaders, referring members to Christian counselors outside the church, or even creating a Christian counseling center as a separate parachurch ministry.

Whether you are in a small church or a large church, you can improve the quality of soul care in your church. Your church is filled with Sarahs and Toms and adults and teenagers with all kinds of issues and problems. Your church can go a long way in helping to meet their needs and to heal their hurts.

> Everything of the believer's life exists within two forms of communion: with the triune God and with other believers. Christians are now co-believers, co-heirs with Christ and joined mystically with all other believers. This leads to acts of love especially manifested in the Church, but this new love is not limited to those in the Church. It is also directed towards those outside the faith, so that they might be drawn into the faith.
>
> —ERIC JOHNSON, *Foundations for Soul Care*

## TRANSFORMATIONAL RELATIONSHIPS

Soul care should take place at every level of a healthy church. This does not mean that everyone deals with the complex, difficult issues in people's lives. It does mean that if the church is fully engaged in soul care at every level rather than tacking it on as just another program, fewer of our people would need counseling, they would grow spiritually, and all of our ministry efforts would be more effective.

Soul care first involves identifying with God's interests in people and their pain. The second key component of soul care is entering into a redemptive relationship with people who are hurting. Transformational growth and healing occur best within the context of community and authentic relationships.

> Two are better than one because they have a good reward for their efforts. For if either falls, his companion can lift him up; but pity the one who falls without another to lift him up. Also, if two lie down together, they can keep warm; but how can one person alone keep warm? And if somebody overpowers one person, two can resist him. A cord of three strands is not easily broken.
> —ECCLESIASTES 4:9-12

According to small-group specialist Rick Howerton, "[Redemptive] groups welcome the fact that life is a series of adventures and battles to face together. When a group of people does life together and doesn't just play at church, people in the group travel the winding gypsy road as a band of brothers and sisters, fully engaged in life and passionate about those on the road with them. They cry on one another's shoulders, laugh together, enjoy the dance, work side-by-side, and go to battle for one another. While life is about the destination, it's even more about the people on the journey."[1] God never designed us for isolation. That's a tactic of our ancient enemy who knows full well that the gates of hell shudder when Christ followers become united as one under the power of our Redeemer.

> We need to develop transformed, empowered disciples who touch our communities.

## A REDEMPTIVE JOURNEY

*Redemption* is defined as "salvation from our sinful state." If that's all it meant, it would be glorious; but that's a narrow definition. Redemption is a far richer concept.

Colossians 1:13-14 shows that we've been forgiven and saved from sin, but beyond that we've been ransomed, rescued, and restored. "[The Father] has rescued us from the domain of darkness and transferred us into the kingdom of the Son He loves, in whom we have redemption, the forgiveness of sins." As believers, God has rescued us and transferred us into Christ's eternal kingdom, but He never promised that our lives in this world would be without hardship, loss, and sadness. Jesus made clear to His followers that "you will have suffering in this world" (John 16:33). Nonetheless we are invited to follow Jesus, live out the new life He has given, and join His redemptive mission in our world. So redemption becomes an ongoing journey in addition to the single point of regeneration.

---

*Redemption includes:*
- *Ransom and rescue*
- *Regeneration*
- *Renewal and recovery*
- *Recruitment*
- *Restoration*

---

An intriguing metaphor that illustrates redemption is that of a father and an adopted child. Romans 8:14-17 summarizes this relationship: "All those led by God's Spirit are God's sons. For you did not receive a spirit of slavery to fall back into fear, but you received the Spirit of adoption, by whom we cry out, 'Abba, Father!' The Spirit Himself testifies together with our spirit that we are God's children, and if children, also heirs—heirs of God and co-heirs with Christ—seeing that we suffer with Him so that we may also be glorified with Him."

When a couple adopts a child, monetary and other costs are nothing short of a *ransom*. The new family *rescues* the child from a life of pain and, in many cases, from death. The child is immediately received into the family and given a new identity (akin to *regeneration*). The child is *restored* to a position as a favored son or daughter and given the full rights of other children in the family. Yet, with all of this, the child still brings issues, doubts, and a lot of baggage from his or her preadoption life. *Renewal* and *recovery* do not come immediately; time is required to heal and reorient the newly adopted child's mind and heart. As the child grows into this new life, experiencing deeper renewal and recovery, he or she is invited or *recruited* into the mission of the adoptive parents.

---

*Somewhere we got the crazy idea that people in relation with Jesus never suffer, and we never fall down.*

---

We all struggle at times in life. Many of us have festering emotional or spiritual wounds that have simply been covered over, pushed below the surface. Somewhere we got the crazy idea that people in relation with Jesus never suffer, and we never fall down as we await our fully restored relationship with God. The Bible's message is the opposite: We are "co-heirs with Christ—*seeing that we suffer with Him* so that we may also be glorified with Him. For I consider that the sufferings of this present time are not worth comparing with the glory that is going to be revealed to us" (Rom. 8:17-18, emphasis added).

> In some way that's still a mystery to us, suffering is connected to our future glory as "co-heirs with Christ"; we must embrace [and walk through] our pain.
>
> —RON KECK, *Colossians: Embrace the Mystery*

We live in a fallen world. Each of us lives out our own story and becomes engaged in battles to be fought and won. Enemy forces in the spiritual realm use live ammo, and sometimes we are the walking wounded. We don't know what lies ahead; unexpected twists and turns in our stories catch us by surprise. Sometimes in tragic circumstances, we're deeply wounded or knocked down. The apostle Paul captured this well:

> *We have this treasure [God's light and glory] in clay jars, so that this extraordinary power may be from God and not from us. We are pressured in every way but not crushed; we are perplexed but not in despair; we are persecuted but not abandoned; we are struck down but not destroyed. We always carry the death of Jesus in our body, so that the life of Jesus may also be revealed in our body. For we who live are always given over to death because of Jesus, so that Jesus' life may also be revealed in our mortal flesh.*
> —2 CORINTHIANS 4:7-11

Redemption includes our ongoing process of renewal and recovery—what theologians call *sanctification*. We dare not take this journey alone; we need deep connection with God and with other people taking the redemptive journey.

## A REDEMPTIVE MISSION

Our redemptive call or recruitment is clearly captured in 2 Corinthians 1:3-5,7: "Blessed be the God and Father of our Lord Jesus Christ, the Father of mercies and the God of all comfort. He comforts us in all our affliction, so that we may be able to comfort those who are in any affliction, through the comfort we ourselves receive from God. For as the sufferings of Christ overflow to us, so our comfort overflows through Christ. . . . And our hope for you is firm, because we know that as you share in the sufferings, so you will share in the comfort."

Jesus pointed back to Isaiah 61:1-3 to identify His redemptive mission. This passage sums up the aim of a soul-care ministry.

> The Spirit of the Lord GOD is on Me,
> because the LORD has anointed Me
> to bring good news to the poor.
> He has sent Me to heal the brokenhearted,
> to proclaim liberty to the captives,
> and freedom to the prisoners;
> to proclaim the year of the LORD's favor,
> and the day of our God's vengeance;
> to comfort all who mourn,
> to provide for those who mourn in Zion;
> to give them a crown of beauty instead of ashes,
> festive oil instead of mourning,
> and splendid clothes instead of despair.
> And they will be called righteous trees,
> Planted by the LORD,
> To glorify Him.
>
> —ISAIAH 61:1-3

This redemptive mission includes all the aspects of our own redemption: ransom and rescue, regeneration, renewal and recovery, recruitment to mission, and restoration—both now and for eternity. We have the awesome privilege of joining Jesus in this adventure!

> We have the awesome privilege of joining Jesus in the adventure of a lifetime—His redemptive mission.

Typical of God's mysteries, we need to lay down our lives to save them. We need to serve to find rest, suffer to receive glory, and help another person find healing in order to further our own healing. William Barclay once wrote, "Love always involves responsibility, and love always involves sacrifice. And we do not really love Christ unless we are prepared to face His task and to take up His cross." God wants to heal and to free us just so we can live abundantly, but He also invites us to take our relationship with Him to the next level.

Have you thought about His (God) handling of the gospel?
God needs to get a message out to the human race, without
which they will perish . . . forever. What's the plan? First,
He starts with the most unlikely group ever: . . . a few
fishermen with no better than a second-grade education, a
tax collector. Then, he passes the ball to us. Unbelievable.

—John Eldredge, *Wild at Heart*

## Purpose of Soul Care

In addition to healing and redemption in peoples' lives, Christ-centered
soul care strengthens community in the local church and also supports other
ministries when special needs arise among the congregation. People performing
soul care in the local church range from the Sunday School teacher to the
Christian professional counselor. All members of the local church should be
receiving and giving soul care to some degree.

Soul care should take place in every ministry venue in the local church.
D. L. Moody once said, "If people only knew how they might cheer some lonely
heart and lift up some drooping spirit, or speak some word that shall be lasting
in its effects for all coming time, they would be up and about it."

> *I give you a new commandment: love one another. Just as I have*
> *loved you, you must also love one another. By this all people will*
> *know that you are My disciples, if you have love for one another.*
> —John 13:34-35

God has appointed certain people for more intensive soul care
within the congregation—people whose experience, gifting, character, or
maturity demonstrate an example for others to follow (1 Cor. 11:1; 1 Tim.
3:1-13; Titus 1:5-9; 1 Pet. 5:1-5; Heb. 13:15-16; Rom. 12:1; 1 Pet. 4:10-11). Each
of us must nurture our personal walk with Christ and influence others as God
providentially places them in our lives. This is the work of soul care at its most
basic level.

---

*Each of us must nurture our personal walk with Christ and*
*influence others as God providentially places them in our lives.*

---

People who are best suited for this work would rather disciple people than lead a program. Let me be clear: there's nothing wrong with programs and events to bring people to the church, and many in the church have special gifting to plan and implement them. However, the people with a burden for the lost and hurting and the desire to focus on the quality of Christian life, rather than the quantity of people drawn to the church, are the ones that should focus on soul care.

## SOUL CARE IS MORE THAN COUNSELING

The foundational concept of soul care is different from counseling. Secular professional counseling is built on a clinical model, supporting professional therapists who operate from models of understanding pain and suffering that do not include the spiritual realm, sin in our world, or God's redemption. Secular professional counseling also assumes the ability to heal people's deep wounds based on clinical models and expertise that are antithetical to the Bible's view of God, man, and healing. This model is often at odds with that of the local church.

> *Christian professional soul care supports and strengthens the local church*

Christian professional counseling as a vital element of soul care, on the other hand, treats pain and suffering with a model that's rich in theology and Christian tradition. It uses God's divinely powerful weapons (2 Cor. 10:4-5) and resources of Christian community (Rom. 15:1; Gal. 6:1-2). It uses the Bible as its ultimate authority to understand and address human pain and suffering. This methodology emphasizes relationship, the indwelling life of Christ, and the sanctifying work of the Holy Spirit. Professional soul-care practitioners believe the best environment for healing is within a healthy Christian community. Christian professional soul care supports and strengthens the local church.

NOTES

1. Rick Howerton, *Destination: Community* (Nashville: Serendipity by LifeWay, 2007), 26.

# CHAPTER 3

# WHY CHURCHES
*Need*
# SOUL-CARE
## MINISTRY

Our kingdom is not of this world, but we have a responsibility to its people, to work for their good, to fight for their souls.

—Bob Briner and Lawrence Kimbrough, *Men in Leadership*

*When [Jesus] saw the crowds, He felt compassion for them, because they were weary and worn out, like sheep without a shepherd.*
—Matthew 9:36

Soul care benefits people in our churches and communities who have specific needs. Some churches see the need and have the vision to go deeper. They focus on developing intense relationships among members and equipping them through intensive, relevant Bible study. Church members, pastors, and leaders meet to discuss problems and discover solutions God has placed in their midst. The focus is on preventing wrong choices and providing a safe place of support and correction. Churches benefit by involving laypeople in ministry and helping them grow as disciples, loving God while serving one another. There is a sense of community, belonging, and support. Within this type of environment, individuals begin to move toward producing spiritual depth and the ability to weather the storms of life.

Many men, women, and even children are self-medicating their pain and loneliness with their drug of choice—entertainment, food, alcohol, drugs, pornography, fantasy or emotional affairs, work, technology, and the list goes on. The church should help people fill the deepest longings of their souls. However, most churches are ill equipped to provide healing, heart transformation, relational intimacy, and a passionate mission; we resort to more labor-intensive programs, more teaching on "just say no" behavior modification and sin management. People have abandoned the search or just can't find the way to intimacy with God.

> The gospel is the proclamation of free love, the revelation of the boundless charity of God. Nothing less than this will suit our world; nothing else is so likely to touch the heart, to go down to the lowest depths of depraved humanity, as the assurance that the sinner has been loved; loved by God; loved with a righteous love; loved with a free love that makes no bargains as to merit, of fitness, or goodness.
>
> —HORATIO BONAR, *God's Way of Holiness*

While the modern church may stand in doctrinal orthodoxy, we no longer deal with the mess or mystery of the soul. Do we have the tools and the courage to take our hurting brothers and sisters to the place where they can be redeemed and God can be glorified? We must learn to open our souls to the people who sit beside us week after week in church. Consider the people who sit beside you in Sunday School, in worship, or at some church program. What kinds of problems might they have? How many people know others well enough to know their problems? If other people knew their problems, would they do anything about them? Most of us don't even know where to start.

In practice we should constantly be reminding ourselves who we are. We need to learn to talk to ourselves, and ask ourselves questions: "Don't you know? Don't you know the meaning of conversion and baptism? Don't you know that you have been united to Christ in his death and resurrection? Don't you know that you have been enslaved to God and have committed yourself to his obedience? Don't you know these things? Don't you know who you are?" We must go on pressing ourselves with such questions, until we reply to ourselves, "Yes, I do know who I am, a new person in Christ, and by the grace of God I shall live accordingly."

—JOHN STOTT, *Romans: God's Good News for the World*

## EXCESSIVE COUNSELING DEMAND

Church growth is good. Bringing more people into the church family, working to expand the kingdom of God, is one of the key functions of the church. When people come to faith in Christ, they bring their emotional and spiritual issues. Even those who have been in the faith for a long time carry deep wounds that have never fully healed. And all of us periodically experience times of difficulty and suffering.

Pastors face an ever-increasing demand from their congregations. Pain and suffering are equal-opportunity offenders. Our brothers and sisters in Christ suffer and need comfort from their spiritual family. Most pastors are not prepared for this overwhelming need, nor do they have time to meet with each suffering member of the church. They soon realize that preaching alone does not alleviate the pain and problems many are confronting.

Many seminaries and training institutions do not prepare pastors for the extensive need among those within the church. Ministers need training that is effective, concise, and consistent in caring for the souls in the local church. Soul care ought to be consistent doctrinally and theologically with the pulpit message, and it should multiply the pastor's effectiveness. A pastor is not hired; he is called, and he needs training to shepherd, lead, and equip.

Pastors gradually realize that as their congregations grow, so does the demand for counseling. Church members need help, and many who suffer expect their pastor to be available. However, many pastors simply don't have the time or ability to meet the soul-care needs of the church. Every church has people at different ages and stages of life. Dealing with children, youth, singles, unwed mothers, adults, marrieds, divorcees, older adults, and people with special mental and physical needs requires a breadth and depth of training that no one person will master. The pastor of a small church may suffer the most. The small congregation that expects the pastor to be a jack-of-all-trades is setting him up for failure. Our ministers grow weary; they have families of their own and require care just like the rest of us.

Some pastors, with the help of church leaders, determine to hire another staff member to take over the counseling need. While another staff member may be a crucial and important step, he or she may soon be overwhelmed by the sheer volume of needs, as well as the variety and complexity of the needs. A minister hired for just such a position said, "All I do is triage and refer people to professionals outside the church."

## HOPE IN A DIFFERENT MODEL OF MINISTRY

All of us, not just pastors, have responsibility in the care and healing of souls. This is what we read in Scripture, but we need to apply what we know. All Christ followers are called to the work of ministry. All the saints should be doing works of service (Eph. 4:11-16).

> [Jesus] personally gave some to be apostles, some prophets, some evangelists, some pastors and teachers, for the training of the saints in the work of ministry, to build up the body of Christ, until we all reach unity in the faith and in the knowledge of God's Son, growing into a mature man with a stature measured by Christ's fullness. Then we will no longer be little children, tossed by the waves and blown around by every wind of teaching, by human cunning with cleverness in the techniques of deceit. But speaking the truth in love, let us grow in every way into Him who is the head—Christ. From Him the whole body, fitted and knit together by every supporting ligament, promotes the growth of the body for building up itself in love by the proper working of each individual part.
>
> —EPHESIANS 4:11-17

The pastor is instructed to equip the saints to do the work, not to do all the work of ministry for the saints. Churches that have inverted God's design do not provide a place of service for the saints, which places their pastors in difficult, if not impossible, situations. Our purpose must be, through the living Scriptures and living Spirit of God, to recover the local church as the authoritative institution for people's sanctification and as the vehicle for their healing and transformation.

The following diagram illustrates this flow of ministry.

## SOUL CARE IN THE CONGREGATION

**PASTORAL
VISION CASTING**
*Motivation, Pulpit
Messages, Leadership*

↓

**SOUL CARE WITHIN
ONGOING
CHURCH MINISTRIES**

↕

**CHURCHWIDE
SOUL-CARE
INITIATIVES**
*Events for Discipleship, Marriage,
Family, etc.*

CONGREGATIONAL
INREACH ←

COMMUNITY
OUTREACH →

Prevention
- - - - - - - -
Intervention

↕

**TARGETED
SOUL-CARE
MINISTRY**
*Topic-Specific Groups
and
Strategic Discipleship*

↕

**MINISTER
RESPONDING
TO CRISES**
*Pastoral Counseling, Conciliation,
Intervention, and Guidance*

↕

**PROFESSIONAL SOUL-CARE MINISTRY**

# EFFECTIVE SOUL CARE AND HEALTHY CHURCHES

An effective soul-care ministry consists of pastors and laity who work together, plan, pray, and maintain a sense of redemptive community. Effective soul care is carefully woven throughout each ministry and fully supports the body of Christ. Both members of the congregation and people in the community are welcomed, loved, and maintain involvement in the local church.

The scriptural church model works. A pastor loves and is loved by the congregation. A congregation supports the pastor in his call to equip believers and put them to work. Hurting people in a community seek out church members equipped to help them and, as a result, end up as a part of the church body. Hurting people are met at their point of need and mature to the point of joining Jesus in His ministry. People help our Lord lay hands on hearts of hurting people for the glory of God and the advancement of His kingdom. This is what soul care is all about—light, freedom, hope, and life.

> *A healthy church must engage members to care for the souls within its community.*

Pain, brokenness, and woundedness are the great equalizers. These experiences break down our pride and defensive structures and make us prime candidates for the love and support of God lived through other Christ followers. We may come to faith as individuals, but we grow in community. The Bible narrative interweaves the stories of individuals and the stories of their spiritual communities. Support, forgiveness, or encouragement within our family of faith gives us the opportunity to draw new life from Jesus as we do life together.

A healthy church must engage in more than providing opportunities to receive information or an emotional experience. A healthy church must engage members to care for the souls within its community. Intimacy and authenticity must be evident among us if we are to bear the image of the One who made us. We only find our lives by losing them for Jesus' sake. We are to be converted from a life of rugged individualism to a life of community when we become Christ followers.

> *Whoever wants to save his life will lose it, but whoever loses his life because of Me and the gospel will save it.*
> —MARK 8:35

> *As we begin the work of soul care, we can create points of ministry.*

The great news is that, as we begin the work of soul care, we can create points of ministry for those whose pain has been transformed into victorious purpose for the kingdom of God. The Bible teaches that caring for the needs of people is the responsibility of the entire congregation.

*Leadership is a gift of service to the body of Christ.*

Hurting people in our churches and communities desperately need well-equipped pastors and lay leaders to provide transformational discipleship that takes place naturally in soul-care venues and supports the preaching and teaching from the pulpit. We need leaders who seek neither to run to the spotlight or to the corner but seek only the place God wants them to be. Leadership is a gift of service to the body of Christ. Leaders do what needs to be done even when they don't know exactly what to do. They help others get where they need to go because they're honest about their own journeys. Leaders in soul care show the love of God and present the truth of God so the Spirit of God will reveal the concern and healing of God in the lives of those in pain.

The Bible clearly calls us all to be ministers and agents of transformation within a community of believers. This is soul care at its core. A church cannot be healthy without it.

The church can often be the worst at expecting more of us than God has called us to shoulder. No is an acceptable answer. A life out of balance will eventually erupt in an explosion of blame, excuses, and frustration.

—BOB BRINER AND LAWRENCE KIMBROUGH, *Men in Leadership*

# CHAPTER 4

# THE BEST
# MODEL
## *for*
# SOUL CARE

We were entertaining people as a substitute for leading them into the presence of God. . . . We didn't need to tweak our methodology, we needed a *modelectomy*.

—WALT KALLESTAD, "'SHOWTIME!' NO MORE," *Leadership Journal*

*Are you hurting? Pray. Do you feel great? Sing. Are you sick? Call the church leaders together to pray and anoint you with oil in the name of the Master. Believing-prayer will heal you, and Jesus will put you on your feet. And if you've sinned, you'll be forgiven—healed inside and out. Make this your common practice: Confess your sins to each other and pray for each other so that you can live together whole and healed. The prayer of a person living right with God is something powerful to be reckoned with.*

JAMES 5:13-16, *The Message*

# A Comprehensive View of Soul Care

Soul care should take place at every level of ministry in a healthy church. The church should be fully engaged in soul care within each ministry venue rather than tacking it on as just another program. Just as physical health care is comprehensive, so is soul care. We cannot loosely approach people's pain, loss, and suffering without a structured biblical mind-set. A redemptive community must be coordinated and the different parts working together for the good of the body (1 Cor. 12:12-26). Soul care involves identifying with God's interests in people and their pain and then entering into a redemptive relationship with them for individual and collective healing and transformation to the glory of God and His kingdom.

> *Soul care at every level of a healthy church:*
> 1. *Identifying with God's interest in people and their pain*
> 2. *Entering into a redemptive relationship with people*

Too often we think: *We have an issue to address; let's create a group or ministry for that.* Our perspective should change so we accept that we're all called to be ministers of transformation. We've all been hurt or wounded, and we all need ongoing redemption. Here are six principles providing a focused approach for effective and safe soul care:

1. Soul care should take place at every level of ministry in a healthy church.
2. Ecclesiastical oversight of soul care is required and provides continuity.
3. Heart transformation occurs in a ministry model, not a secular managed-care structure (see section 4).
4. Soul care must be Christ centered, Spirit directed, and biblically grounded.
5. Proper structures and operating procedures provide strong liability protection.
6. Training and accountability are required for all soul-care workers.

Soul care and healing should be the underpinning of all we do in the church. We're instructed to take the good news to a lost and hurting world and to make disciples of all nations. We're to share the good news of abundant life in the present and for all eternity. The cure of our souls rests in a new life through a real and vital relationship with our Lord Jesus Christ. The care of our souls rests in our communal and relational journey with our brothers and sisters in the present day as we await the glory we are promised. We've already established that we cannot escape the broken world in which we live or the broken vessels we occupy.

This model assumes that the pastor is the spiritual leader, the shepherd of the church, and that he is the one who will lead the church in developing the

# Comprehensive Soul Care

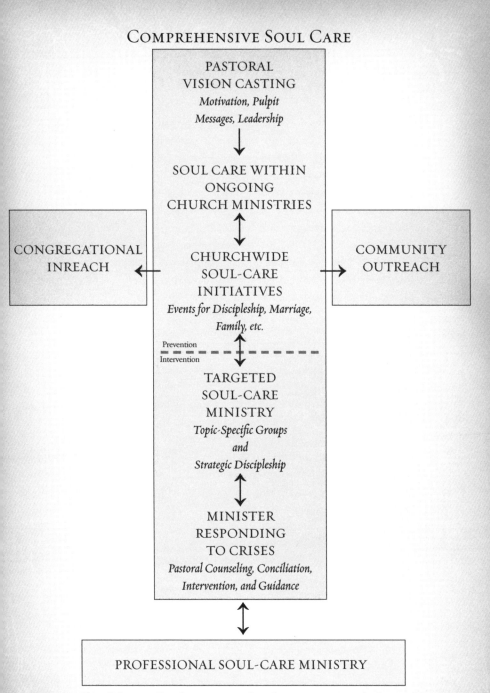

PASTORAL
VISION CASTING
*Motivation, Pulpit
Messages, Leadership*

SOUL CARE WITHIN
ONGOING
CHURCH MINISTRIES

CHURCHWIDE
SOUL-CARE
INITIATIVES
*Events for Discipleship, Marriage,
Family, etc.*

Prevention
Intervention

TARGETED
SOUL-CARE
MINISTRY
*Topic-Specific Groups
and
Strategic Discipleship*

MINISTER
RESPONDING
TO CRISES
*Pastoral Counseling, Conciliation,
Intervention, and Guidance*

CONGREGATIONAL
INREACH

COMMUNITY
OUTREACH

PROFESSIONAL SOUL-CARE MINISTRY

structure for all forms of soul care. Most churches may agree with this in theory, but their ministry efforts are often fragmented and are not consistent with the pastor's vision for the flock. An integrated model draws the church together and gives continuity in the mission and message of redemption in Jesus.

# CONTINUITY OF SOUL-CARE COMPONENTS

Soul care always has five inseparable, strategically directed components. Through these components, leadership is multiplied, community is strengthened, lives are transformed, and we're all better for it.

1. PREVENTION works strategically and intentionally to build relationships and lead people on a transformational journey with God.
2. INTERVENTION occurs when problems become apparent, crises arise, and special attention is necessary to restore individuals and families.
3. INTERCESSORY MINISTRY recognizes that none of our soul-care efforts will be effective if God doesn't show up. We need His presence and power for transformation and healing.
4. PASTORAL COUNSELING provides a deeper level of intervention for people in need of biblical or spiritual direction and occurs in almost all churches.
5. PROFESSIONAL COUNSELING supports the church in soul-care intervention through handling more acute or urgent issues.

# PROACTIVE PREVENTION

The church should be intentional about preaching, teaching, and training from the Word of God to a world seeking freedom, joy, and peace. God loves us and is not some cosmic killjoy. When He says, "You shall not," He's doing that for our protection and to prevent us from experiencing or causing painful consequences. He is trying to *prevent* His children from experiencing pain and suffering just as our parents tried to prevent us from making decisions that would hurt us or others.

Prevention in this model requires that we don't settle for just proclaiming propositional truth. Beyond solely reading, studying, and dissecting the Bible, becoming a disciple of Christ involves unifying knowledge with experience—living it out in the reality of our relationships.

> *Proactive soul care must be relational.*

It's not enough that we know intellectual propositions. If it were, our Western world would be brimming with enthusiastic, effective disciples for Christ. And our world would be changed. We must first apply that truth personally and then experience the presence and power of God. Then we will begin to understand, embrace, and live out that truth interdependently. Ministry means that we are interacting, depending, providing, and sharing life's ups and downs with one another. As we think of ministry (the act of service), all the services we provide impact the souls we touch. Since we're all ministers doing ministry, we have abundant opportunities to serve or care for souls.

There are as many venues for soul care as there are ministries in your church. Examples include pulpit ministry, home groups, Sunday School, discipleship training, marriage and family ministry, youth and children's ministry, seniors ministry, men's ministry, and women's ministry. Proactive soul care must be relational but can take place in special large-group events, small groups, or in one-on-one discipleship. By expressing the truth of God to the people of God, based on their willingness to hear and obey, many sorrows may be prevented. This is soul care at its most basic level.

Proactive soul care depends on a mind-set. Teaching the Word of God and establishing authentic and meaningful relationships go a long way to protect people, prepare them to make good choices, and teach them to walk in the presence and power of God. Lay leaders need to broaden their roles as disciplers to include being soul-care providers. Group leaders can shift mind-sets to help group members accept their role in being healing agents who help one another find spiritual transformation and healing.

## THE POWER OF COMMUNITY IN SOUL CARE

Some would say that people in churches are the loneliest and most isolated we've ever been. The more we tolerate individualism in our congregations, the more isolated we become. We need to move from independence to interdependence.

Living within an authentic, redemptive community is necessary to experience the fullness of God's relational plan for us. A preventive focus in soul care works strategically and intentionally to build authentic relationships. Our culture promotes *independence*. The body of Christ is commanded to promote and support *interdependence* on our Lord and on one another (Phil. 2:1-4). Individuals and families go through similar life-stage transitions that are often overlooked, ignored, or neglected by the modern church. Ministries are often fragmented, working independently, resulting in a lack of community and a burden on our families. Our culture has permeated the church, and we need one another in our battles against "the lust of the flesh, the lust of the eyes, and the pride in one's lifestyle" (1 John 2:16).

> *If then there is any encouragement in Christ, if any consolation of love, if any fellowship with the Spirit, if any affection and sympathy, fulfill my joy by thinking the same way, having the same love, sharing the same feelings, focusing on one goal. Do nothing out of rivalry or conceit, but in humility consider others as more important than yourselves. Everyone should look not only for his own interests, but also for the interests of others.*
> —PHILIPPIANS 2:1-4

A resourceful preventative focus may include mentoring relationships, specialized short-term, small-group Bible studies, Christian education courses, ministry education, and specialized retreats. Additionally, an effective preventative approach will connect and unite other ministries in the local church. Crucial times in the life of congregants such as weddings, first child, child entering adolescence, empty nest, blending families, and caring for family members are opportunities for the church to instruct, sustain, and model godly relationships. A preventive soul-care ministry will invest in individuals, couples, and parents during life-stage transitions and difficult times to support and uphold the health of the family.

Well-designed soul care will strengthen intergenerational relationships within the family and church. Many families attend church, and each person goes his or her own way, seldom interacting during any worship or church functions. Children and young adults are disadvantaged by not having deep connections with the older generation in the church and vice versa. We should not ignore Paul's instructions in Titus 2. It's important for families to interact, encourage, and connect spiritually with other families, not just one individual to another. An emphasis on prevention will work to coordinate all these ministries so that the body works together as one large family where holiness and unity are promoted, discipleship is the norm, and the lost are called to Christ.

> Instead of counting the people and the offerings, now we look for evidence that people are breaking out of their private, cocooned lives and are fully engaged with God and serving Him. We want them to do more than grab a cup of coffee in the lobby or meet someone new during worship gatherings. We want them to go deep with one another.
>
> —Walt Kallestad, " 'Showtime!' No More," *Leadership Journal*

## INTERVENTION

Sometimes, for reasons we are not meant to understand, bad things happen to us even when our fellowship with God is at its strongest. We experience loss and suffer even when we feel that we've done everything right. God is there to bring us back, to *intervene*; He expects His people to join Him in this task.

We also see those who did not listen to God's admonitions and suffered greatly. The nation of Israel wanted earthly kings like other nations; they wanted to worship many gods like other nations, and they often suffered greatly for their disobedience. The good news is that when God's chosen people suffered, He eventually rescued them. He *intervened* when they suffered by no fault of their own and even when they would not listen!

Effective intervention is designed to take those who, for whatever reason, are in a crisis and lead them back into the family of God. It moves them through the crisis so they can reestablish themselves back into the "prevention" aspect of soul care. In medicine people who suffer a health crisis receive emergency or intensive care often followed by some form of rehabilitation. Then they're able to reestablish themselves back into the normal flow of their daily lives. This is also the dynamic in soul care. Our emergency or intensive care occurs in topic-specific groups, pastoral counseling, intensive remedial discipleship, and professional soul care. All of these venues are designed to move people back into the body to participate in worship, fellowship, and ministry to prevent others from experiencing the same crisis they survived. The cycle of biblical soul care meets the needs of all people in all stages of life and keeps them active in doing life together.

> *I do not do the good that I want to do, but I practice the evil that I do not want to do. Now if I do what I do not want to do, I am no longer the one doing it, but it is the sin that lives in me.*
> —Romans 7:19-20

## Straightforward Intervention— an Effective, Simple Model

I've provided five descriptive categories of need that may prove to be helpful. Based on our discussion of prevention and intervention, areas 1-4 can generally be covered through transformational community and the teaching/discipleship activities in the church—*prevention*. Area 5 usually requires *intervention* as do issues in areas 1-4 that become acute and create a crisis for individuals or families.

People consistently demonstrate five areas of need.
1. SIN. Believers engage in remnant sin, while unbelievers deal with reigning sin.
2. CONFUSION. God's people frequently need clarification on issues regarding God, grace, suffering, prayer, relationships, social role of the believer, and so on. False beliefs and vows can play a large role in this area.
3. HURT. Believers experience hurt through rejection, loss, betrayal, etc., and need ministry.
4. CONFLICT. Members need to resolve conflicts between them. This includes conflicts between husband and wife, parent and child, member and member, and so on. Conflicts are often the result of resentment, bitterness, unforgiveness, blocked goals, selfishness, and related causes.
5. MEDICAL OR PSYCHOLOGICAL ILLNESS. These needs usually require professional intervention for stabilization.

What does all this mean and what does it have to do with soul care in the church? It means the church is loosening from her biblical roots and, in doing so, is losing the power to touch the depth of the real needs of the human soul. What can we do about this? I think we can begin by doing two things: (1) refocusing the church's ministry through the gospel lens; and (2) reclaiming the blessing of bearing one another's burdens.

—Pastor Tony Rose

## Levels of Issue Severity and Intervention

Most of the needs mentioned above are addressed within the context of normal ministerial activity such as preaching, teaching, and special events. Trained church staff and laity can appropriately deal with most of these needs. However, when these needs become chronic or more intense, it might be necessary to refer to topic-specific healing groups or pastoral counseling for more in-depth spiritual guidance. Finally, when needs are severe or begin greatly to affect a person's ability to function, referral to a professional might be appropriate. Staff and leadership training is necessary to ensure that appropriate interventions take place.

> *The dynamics of community, relationship, and interdependence are sorely lacking in many churches today.*

The Picking Up the Pieces study series is designed primarily to support the areas of established need that include sin, confusion, hurt, and conflict by providing topic-specific groups or individual soul care. The effectiveness of professional soul care is enhanced when the counselee attends these groups. We should applaud the efforts of churches that have implemented topic-specific intervention groups to meet the hurting at their point of need and love them enough not to let them stay there. These groups provide a valuable function, teaching participants to confront pain and crises in biblical fashion. They build a sense of community, relationship, and interdependence. These dynamics are sorely lacking in many of our churches today. As long as the content of these groups is doctrinally sound and Christ honoring, members grow in their faith, their value to the kingdom, and their value to one another.

Soul care in topic-specific groups will draw people from the community and direct them into the church body. These groups will reach into the church serving as a resource for church members. Individuals participating in these groups seldom attend just one group. For example, a person struggling with grief will often discover that unforgiveness is an issue they have not dealt with adequately. As individuals move into the church body over time and mature in their faith, they will often be burdened to lead a group. These groups serve as a resource for the pastor and leaders in the church.

> I give you a new commandment: love one another. Just as I have loved you, you must also love one another. By this all people will know that you are My disciples, if you have love for one another.
> —JOHN 13:34-35

## LET'S RISK INTERVENING!

We should view an effective soul-care ministry as a matrix intersecting with other ministries in the church. A ministry with a strong intervention component will be a resource for people who need more strategic and urgent care. These interventions can be conducted individually, as a family, or in small-group settings. Additionally, intervention will direct congregants into appropriate mentoring relationships, small groups, and courses that address specific topics that would be helpful in the long run. Last but not least, interventional soul care will assist individuals and families in selecting ministries to promote harmony and meet their specific needs when problems arise. For instance, if a husband is struggling with an addiction, the soul-care ministry would also assist the wife and children with ministries that meet their needs at that time. Another example is when teens experience trouble or trauma; the soul-care ministry would support the teen *and* the parents with appropriate ministry efforts.

An intentional soul-care ministry will promote a sense of community and strengthen the relationships God has ordained within the church. Its purpose is to bring about growth, healing, and sanctification in order to bring greater glory to God and His kingdom through His people (Rom. 15:1-4). A healthy church family gives each member the opportunity to love and be loved, to serve and be served, to admonish and be admonished, to celebrate and be celebrated. An effective soul-care ministry will be strong in both prevention and intervention.

# CHAPTER 5

# THE
# PROFESSIONAL
## *Soul-Care*
# COMPONENT

People are uncomfortable with mystery (God) and mess (themselves). They avoid both mystery and mess by devising programs and hiring pastors to manage them. A program provides a defined structure with an achievable goal. Mystery and mess are eliminated at a stroke. This is appealing. In the midst of the mysteries of grace and the complexities of human sin, it is nice to have something that you can evaluate every month or so and find out where you stand. We don't have to deal with ourselves or with God, but can use the vocabulary of religion and work in an environment that acknowledges God, and so be assured that we are doing something significant.

—EUGENE PETERSON, *The Contemplative Pastor*

*I will lead the blind by a way they did not know; I will guide them on paths they have not known. I will turn darkness to light in front of them, and rough places into level ground. This is what I will do for them, and I will not forsake them.*
—ISAIAH 42:16

# PROFESSIONAL SOUL-CARE INTERVENTION

Professional intervention occurs when problems become apparent, crises arise, and special attention is necessary to restore individuals and families to health that is beyond the scope of laypersons' training. Yes, intervention takes place in both pastoral and professional venues; but the pastor should see the professional as part of the team who assists him in keeping the sheep from straying from the church. Intervention must always have the intent of keeping those receiving special help engaged in the church. The professional should seek the counselee's authorization to communicate with the pastoral staff ensuring that professional and ministry efforts are coordinated.

Even small churches can effectively engage in soul-care intervention. The Picking Up the Pieces materials and leadership training provided in section 2 equip church leaders and members with a structure to support and nourish people in the middle of difficult and painful struggles. Trained, gifted, and experienced individuals can intervene and nourish those who are hurting for whatever reason. The pastoral staff can make use of available resources (see forms in section 3) and seek professionals who are like-minded when the severity of problems overreaches the training of those involved in ministry-based soul care.

# PROFESSIONAL SOUL-CARE OPTIONS
# FOR LARGER AND SMALLER CHURCHES

The professional counseling relationships in any church's soul-care ministry are vitally important since a significant portion of any church's congregation will experience unexpected loss, medical problems, and/or psychological problems that require trained intervention. Some members receiving professional help might be ashamed or feel spiritually weak because they are seeking help outside the church. The church can do much to assist in the care of damaged souls and deal with this stigma by adopting structures that serve those with special needs.

Three safe and effective approaches will serve your church well.

### APPROACH 1. PASTORAL REFERRAL TO PROFESSIONAL CHRISTIAN COUNSELORS.

Pastors typically refer to professionals. In smaller churches pastors usually refer to someone they've met, someone with a good reputation within the Christian community, or someone recommended by another pastor. I have urged all pastors to develop a questionnaire and set up a meeting time with counseling professionals in the community. They need to ask the hard questions: "How do you counsel? Do you use the Bible in your counseling? What do you believe about divorce? Where did you go to school/seminary? Tell me about your faith and how it impacts your work," and so forth. It's ideal in these situations when the professional is a member of the same church or a sister church. However, this is not always the case.

Pastors need to understand that they have more influence among Christian professionals than they may realize. One of my board members is the executive pastor of a large church. He recently identified several licensed professionals in his congregation and developed a relationship with them and introduced them to the Christ-centered counselors in our ministry. Perhaps over time these counselors may be willing to submit fully to ecclesiastical oversight, which takes them to the strongest model.

A Christian psychologist, counselor, or mental health worker depends on referrals to make his or her living, and reputation is critical. Church leaders need to see this as an opportunity to develop relationships with these people and, over time, influence them toward a more biblical methodology. (A counselor interview form is included in section 3 for your use.)

> *Pastors need to ask professional counselors the hard questions and use their influence well.*

**APPROACH 2. PROFESSIONAL SOUL CARE—A FULL-ORBED MODEL UNDER ECCLESIASTICAL AUTHORITY**. This is the best model, but it is not realistic for smaller churches. The ideal is for the church to develop another not-for-profit entity to provide professional soul care. The separate parachurch organization would be accountable to a board of directors from the host church to provide oversight and maintain financial integrity. This model accomplishes the best of both worlds while protecting the church from risk or liability.

When the church and the professional counseling entity work in tandem, we have returned the authority back to the local church, we have begun to put pressure on counselors who call themselves Christian (since the church is a primary referral source) to examine their practice from a biblical perspective, and we are directly confronting many of the secular theoretical presuppositions of the counselors. The professional counseling entity should be a Christian organization that ascribes to a distinctly Christian view of God, people, redemption, and transformation. It should be a true *para-* (alongside) church ministry committed to support the local church in training, congregational inreach, and community outreach.

I strongly recommend that the hosting church or churches appoint or elect a board of directors to oversee the operation of the professional soul-care entity to ensure theological and doctrinal integrity. This allows the local church to have appropriate ecclesiastical oversight without legal vulnerability. It ensures members of the local church are receiving counsel that is consistent with a Christian worldview. The professionals in this model should be examined as closely as a staff member would be for the local church. This model coheres spiritually, intellectually, and structurally with every other ministry in the church and aligns with pastoral vision and leadership.

Professional Christian counselors that you would consider for this type of soul-care ministry should answer the following questions affirmatively.

1. Are you willing to submit your theories, methods, and structures to biblical scrutiny?
2. Do you ascribe to a distinctly Christian model of God, people, redemption, and transformation?
3. Are you willing to submit yourself or your practice to the local church's ecclesiastical oversight since you are treating its members?
4. Will you practice in accordance with the clearly stated institutional methodologies of the church or parachurch organization?

For more detailed information on setting up a separate professional counseling entity, go to *www.heartlifesoulcare.org*.

> *The full-orbed model provides the best solution for ecclesiastical oversight and risk management.*

**APPROACH 3. PROFESSIONAL SOUL CARE—A FULL-ORBED MODEL TIED TO MULTIPLE CHURCHES**. Approach 2, with a dedicated professional soul-care entity connected to a single church, requires more resources than most churches possess. However, cooperative measures can make this happen more broadly. Like-minded churches within the same geographical area can band together to create the separate professional counseling entity described in approach 2. For example, HeartLife Professional Soul-Care has four churches represented on our board of directors. A related alternative is for some smaller churches to partner with a church that does have the resources for approach 2, lending resources and assistance as feasible.

This again is the model that brings the church back to its appointed role as God's primary institution of the care and healing of souls. I've worked with many churches over the years using different components of this model. Success and effectiveness in soul care were limited because on some level members in trouble had to go outside the church's authority, and so the care was not as seamless or effective as it could have been. Each church that supports this model of professional soul care will have the ability to influence professionals dedicated to strengthen and grow the body of Christ. This model provides:

- Professional Counseling—Individual, marital, family, and group professional, Christ-centered counseling services
- Access—Professional help available 24-7 when crises arise
- Training Resource—Ongoing support and training for staff and laity

- Ministry Support—Backup and transfer of emergent situations for staff and teachers when church members experience trauma or crisis

This model is accountable, biblical, and influential. It helps the local church in intensive discipleship, topic-specific small groups, or Bible study venues. It provides a resource that reinforces all church members' being able to do the work of ministry at the level they are trained or gifted.

> If you want to be incrementally better: Be competitive.
> If you want to be exponentially better: Be cooperative.

## COORDINATION OF SOUL-CARE COMPONENTS

A church's interventional focus in soul care will coordinate with a church-based professional soul-care ministry (in best case scenarios) or with the pastor and other leaders (in smaller churches) to promote healing of individuals and restore damaged relationships. By having a structure that coordinates these efforts, soul care will have a resource for people who need a more intensive discipleship intervention.

Professional counselors should coordinate with the church by regularly directing their counselees to church resources (worship, Sunday School, life groups, Bible study, topic-specific small groups, and other appropriate discipleship or ministry functions). Professional counselors should move counselees into the church's soul-care ministry when emergent issues are stabilized. Counselors should maintain a strong level of communication (when the counselee gives authorization) regarding the progress of church members referred to counseling. Small-group leaders, mentors, and Sunday School teachers need immediate resources for people in crises. Church leaders can provide strategic discipleship opportunities to enhance church members' spiritual journeys and to prevent problems from reaching crisis situations.

The church needs to consider and support the needs of all family members when a person is going through a difficult time. The soul-care team must assess difficult situations (with the help of professionals as needed) and develop a ministry support plan for all involved. Again, this is most effectively done within the context of the church's full set of ministries so prevention and intervention will be carefully and intentionally coordinated.

Life within the church family should be a sanctifying process, promoting healing and holiness. By being intentional with prevention and intervention, the local church, large or small, will approach this ideal, deeply impacting individuals, couples, and families for Christ. A healthy church family provides strength for the storms of life, wisdom for decisions ahead, accountability for spiritual growth, and a safe place where wounds can be healed.

# CHAPTER 6

# DEVELOPING THE
# VISION AND PLAN
## *for*
# YOUR SOUL-CARE
# MINISTRY

The religious community is essential, for alone our vision is too narrow to see all that must be seen. Together, our vision widens and strength is renewed.

—Mark Morrison-Reed

*Without revelation people run wild, but one who keeps the law will be happy.*

—Proverbs 29:18

Internalizing the need for the church to reclaim soul care and understanding the best model to follow provides most of what you need to create a dynamic soul-care ministry in your church. The transforming and rewarding work of soul care can now begin. The lives of people, families, and your church are at stake, so be intentional, strategic, and wise in setting up your ministry.

- Keep the big picture in mind.
- Create a compelling vision.
- Develop a realistic plan.
- Keep casting the vision to your church
- Balance intervention with prevention.
- Select the right leaders and equip them.
- Give energy and resources to coordination and support.

## KEEP THE BIG PICTURE IN MIND

As you dive into planning your work and working your plan, keep in mind why you're engaging in soul-care ministry. It cannot be just another program. Soul care should take place at every level of ministry in a healthy church. It's about caring, comforting, confronting, and courage-building in the context of authentic relationships and redemptive community.

Soul care involves identifying with God's interests in people and their pain and then entering into a redemptive relationship with them for individual and collective healing and transformation to the glory of God and His kingdom. Jesus' mission captured in Isaiah 61:1-3 is a great place to begin your vision statement.

Recall and review the guiding principles for effective and safe soul care:

1. Soul care should take place at every level of ministry in a healthy church.
2. Ecclesiastical oversight of soul care is required and provides continuity.
3. Heart transformation occurs in a ministry model, not a secular managed-care structure.
4. Soul care must be Christ centered, Spirit directed, and biblically grounded.
5. Good structures and operating procedures provide strong liability protection.
6. Training and accountability are required for all soul-care workers.

## CREATE A COMPELLING VISION

A well-crafted vision statement can be powerful as the rallying point for your ministry. It should paint a picture that creates a sense of passion and builds commitment for attaining your vision.

The vision for your soul-care ministry needs to be integrated with the overall vision and mission of your church. The pastor, along with key leaders, should take the lead in developing this vision. Healing, freedom, and transformation start with the leaders. Seek God and His desires for your church. Saturate everything you do with prayer.

> *Your vision should be:*
>   1. *A concise, compelling picture of the future.*
>   2. *Far-reaching but attainable.*

## DEVELOP A REALISTIC PLAN

Not every church has the same situation or the same resources. Many churches may not be able to execute the full-orbed plan. That's OK! God expects you to follow Him in faith, being good stewards of what He has given you. Implementing some of your long-term vision is far better than sitting still.

Creating a realistic plan in order to achieve your goals is vital. A realistic plan takes into account your current situation and your available resources. You may have a larger plan in mind up the road but take successive steps toward those goals. Taking on more than you can realistically accomplish is a plan for failure, so keep stepping up toward success. Some things can be implemented more quickly than others, and that's great as long as you keep the bigger picture in mind.

> *A realistic plan takes into account your current situation and your available resources.*

In smaller churches the pastor can easily be overwhelmed trying to cover all the soul-care needs on his own. By integrating soul care into the church's ongoing ministries and by training appropriate laity to lead topic-specific intervention groups, the pastor's load will diminish tremendously. Another way laypersons can minister is by providing care for church members in times of crisis.

A few years ago a pastor friend at a small church contacted me because he was overwhelmed by the crises and counseling needs of his congregation. He was essentially on call 24-7. We developed a simple but effective soul-care plan for his church on a napkin in a restaurant.

I suggested he involve deacons and church leaders in ministering to hurting church members. He purchased a pager, and we developed a rotation schedule for a few of his most trusted leaders. Each lay leader carried the pager for three days before passing it to the next person on the rotation. If there were unresolved issues, each leader was responsible to communicate the specifics to the next "on call" layman and the pastor. The current "on call" layman stayed involved if it was best for the member in crisis. Every three days the "on call" layman reported to the pastor and the next man on the rotation. When it was appropriate for a woman to be involved, the "on call" layman included his wife. In any acute situation the pastor was involved immediately.

The next phase of our plan was to select a group of laity who were trained, and the church began six topic-specific groups using Picking Up the Pieces materials. The number and size of these groups grew as leaders learned to refer people who would benefit by participating in the groups. In complex circumstances the pastor would refer to a group of professionals he respected and knew would serve his members and support the church's ministry.

As this church has grown, so have the soul-care efforts. Now that the church is larger, more ministers and laymen are involved in caring for members. Additional benefits to this structure are that the pastor has greater support from his leaders and church ministries are involved in caring for people.

Another approach for smaller churches is to partner with larger churches with multiple staff. The larger church might provide support to smaller churches in the form of training, process development, pastoral counseling, or professional counseling if the larger church has established a separate professional soul-care entity. Be intentional about addressing each area of the comprehensive soul-care model:

- Prevention—incorporating soul care in ongoing church ministries
- Intervention—launching targeted soul-care ministries and topic-specific groups
- Intercession—developing your prayer warriors
- Pastoral counseling—adjusting your current approach as needed
- Professional counseling—creating the best scenario for your church members

Always be sure to pilot, evaluate, and adjust your ideas and approaches before full-scale implementation. You can learn valuable lessons from other churches that are on this journey too.

## KEEP CASTING THE VISION TO YOUR CHURCH

If you want people to join you in making your vision a reality, you have to develop within people a passion for that vision. Like many things in life, this is an ongoing, developing process rather than a one-time splash. Show people how God is moving and how they can play a vital role in the healing, freedom, and transformation that He desires for His people.

> Not everything that counts can be counted,
> and not everything that can be counted counts.
>
> —ALBERT EINSTEIN

## Balance Intervention with Prevention

You may feel the urgency of addressing the needs of people in your church through intervention. That may well be where God would have you focus your initial efforts, but never underestimate the power of the prevention side of soul-care.

> *Give qualified laity the opportunity for a vital point of ministry that will unify the body and make it healthier.*

## Select the Right Leaders and Equip Them

Great groups have great leaders. Churches need to recruit excellent leaders to facilitate soul-care groups. Good administrative leaders may not necessarily be the soul workers you need. The Leadership Training Program in section 2 is designed to help you determine those "A" leaders. Use the training program both to evaluate and to equip leaders for this specific ministry.

> The leaders who work most effectively, it seems to me, never say "I." And that's not because they have trained themselves not to say "I." They don't think "I." They think "we"; they think "team." They understand their job to be to make the team function. They accept responsibility and don't sidestep it, but "we" gets the credit. This is what creates trust, what enables you to get the task done.
>
> —Peter Drucker

## Give Energy and Resources to Coordination and Support

Coordination of the soul-care components will require some time and energy, but you can open an avenue of ministry for trusted laity to help in this area, and the overall effectiveness of your soul-care ministry will serve you, your people, and your church mission well. The same is true for providing support and encouragement to your soul-care leaders.

This kind of ministry can be energizing but also draining at times. Your leaders need authentic, supportive community as much as those who attend the groups they lead. It's much easier to maintain than it is to have to start over. Invest in your leaders so they can invest in others. *For more resources or assistance in planning and implementing your soul-care ministry, visit* www.heartlifesoulcare.org.

# CHAPTER 7

# SELECTING *the* RIGHT LEADERS

If your actions inspire others to dream more, learn more, do more and become more, you are a leader.

—John Quincy Adams

> The instruction of the LORD is perfect,
> reviving the soul;
> the testimony of the LORD is trustworthy,
> making the inexperienced wise. . . .
> Who perceives his unintentional sins?
> Cleanse me from my hidden faults.
> Moreover, keep Your servant from willful sins;
> do not let them rule over me.
> Then I will be innocent,
> and cleansed from blatant rebellion.
> May the words of my mouth
> and the meditation of my heart
> be acceptable to You,
> LORD, my rock and my Redeemer.

—Psalm 19:7,12-14

The key to a successful soul-care ministry is called, competent small-group leaders. Hands-on leadership in the healing process is where the rubber meets the road. I've seen mediocre ministries thrive because of good group leaders, and I've seen wonderfully organized ministries struggle because of selecting the wrong leaders and not equipping them. The people you should talk with about being leaders of your groups should demonstrate adequacy in the areas highlighted in this chapter. More than that, you'd like to see continued progress in these areas. A Leadership Assessment Form is provided in section 3 so you can easily assess the key traits.

## CHARACTERISTICS OF EFFECTIVE SOUL-CARE WORKERS

Christian leaders fully accept that their positions are gifts from God and their influence is dependent on His help. When problems are overwhelming and there are no easy answers, leaders call on God for help and ask for wisdom. They also teach others how to bring problems before the Lord.

> *If any of you lacks wisdom, he should ask God, who gives to all generously and without criticizing, and it will be given to him.*
> —JAMES 1:5

**LEADERS ARE AUTHENTIC AND SERVE GOD'S AGENDA, NOT THEIR OWN.** They genuinely believe God's leadership principles are not true because they work; rather, they work because they are true. In Psalm 26:1-4 David invited God to examine him, to test his integrity. This is a statement of authenticity. Authenticity is a primary requirement for soul workers.

> *May integrity and uprightness keep me, for I wait for You. . . . Vindicate me, LORD, because I have lived with integrity and have trusted in the LORD without wavering. Test me, LORD, and try me; examine my heart and mind. For Your faithful love is before my eyes, and I live by Your truth. I do not sit with the worthless or associate with hypocrites.*
> —PSALM 25:21; 26:1-4

**LEADERS COUNT THE COST (LUKE 14:28-35).** Serving as a soul worker is expensive. It will cost time that would be easier spent elsewhere. Leaders use their time and words carefully. When we have influence over others' lives, the responsibility is overwhelming. The longer we remain in leadership, the greater the personal responsibility.

> *Which of you, wanting to build a tower, doesn't first sit down and calculate the cost to see if he has enough to complete it?*
> —LUKE 14:28

**LEADERS ARE TRUTHFUL, TRANSPARENT, AND TRUSTWORTHY**. Leaders don't pretend. They are real, the persons God made them to be. Facing problems truthfully is the only way to a healthy outcome. Leaders are to be authentic and truthful, and they cannot do this without relationship and community. God created people for relationship and not for isolation.

You cannot help others accept themselves as God made them to be if you hide behind a mask of competence or confidence. If you are dealing with insecure people, you must teach them authenticity by being transparent. Know when to challenge and when to support. Don't hesitate to disclose the hard times you have been through as you stand by those in their times of trouble.

To create a safe environment for sharing, growth, and healing in your group setting, you must be trustworthy. Members must trust your love for them if they are going to invite you along on their journey. They will not be transparent or truthful if they feel you are critical, judgmental, or that you will share their stories with others. Group leaders who are truthful and transparent about their own journeys engender the same quality in others. Remember the rule of the Three T's: No Trust without Truth shared with Transparency.

**LEADERS ARE RELATIONAL**. Leaders recognize the importance of building relationships. If soul-care leaders don't enjoy developing relationships with people, something is wrong. When soul workers feel people are a nuisance, life is out of sync. Leaders are servants. True humility is not passive; humble soul workers recognize their total dependence on God and their highly valuable contribution. Leadership is a gift of service. When leaders don't know what to do, they do what needs to be done. Look for people who have a track record of service.

## CHARACTERISTICS OF EFFECTIVE SOUL-CARE WORKERS

Grace and humility are two concepts I've highlighted throughout this book. Effective soul-care practitioners help others out of an awareness of their personal brokenness. It's critical for all soul-care workers to approach their work with meekness that comes from an awareness of God's grace in their own lives. Otherwise, they may come across harsh and legalistic; they will do more harm than good in the life of the one seeking help.

**A SOUL-CARE WORKER MUST BE HUMBLE**. Nothing in God's kingdom is stronger than humility or weaker than pride. We must always remember that anything begun in self-confidence ends in shame. Humility always overcomes evil with good. There is no good apart from Christ, yet prideful leaders continue in self-willed directions no matter the cost to His bride. Pride, a need to control, arrogance, and anger will draw us to condemn others. Jesus gave His life to wipe out shame and condemnation.

**A SOUL-CARE WORKER MUST BE SELF-AWARE**. Accurate self-awareness is essential for a soul-care worker. Defensiveness and self-protection have no place in the arena of soul care. A soul-care worker helps people release the shame and condemnation Jesus removed from us. A soul-care worker will exemplify this truth: "No condemnation now exists for those in Christ Jesus" (Romans 8:1).

**A SOUL-CARE WORKER MUST UNDERSTAND THE DYNAMICS OF PAIN**. When we're injured, our Christian principles often disappear. Satan works with cunning, speaking and repeating lies to keep us captive and ineffective. He works in the realms of fear, selfishness, and divisiveness. He loves to draw us back into the darkness of shame and condemnation, pointing to our sins, failures, and weaknesses with an accusing finger.

**A SOUL-CARE WORKER MUST BE KNOWLEDGEABLE AND TRUTHFUL ABOUT THE POWER OF SIN**. Each person involved in the ministry of soul care must come to the knowledge that, while we are new creations in Christ, we continue to fight for freedom against the Devil and the sin that dwells in us. The apostle Paul addressed these issues in Romans 7:13-25 and Galatians 5:16-26. Believers today deal with the same struggles as did believers in the early church.

**SOUL-CARE WORKERS MUST BE FAMILIAR WITH GOD'S WORD AND APPLY IT TO THEIR LIVES**. Paul told Timothy and Titus to appoint leaders in the church who exhibited Christlike character (1 Tim. 3:1-13; Titus 1:5-9). Soul-care workers must be aware of the issues in their own lives as revealed by the Holy Spirit through the Word of God.

**SOUL-CARE WORKERS DOES NOT DISTORT THE CHARACTER OR AGENDA OF GOD**. We must be careful that we do not use our personal dispositions to justify a distortion of any of God's characteristics. The primary responsibility of anyone called into the ministry of soul care is to identify with God's interests in the lives of those who need help; we must align with God's agenda in the lives of others. We are to maintain transparency and truth within the community of our fellow soul workers. We must maintain a passionate and authentic relationship with God. We must constantly and consistently ask the Holy Spirit to search our hearts and apply the "law of the Lord" to our own lives. We must allow Him constantly to restore our souls if we are to be effective in leading others to healing and transformation.

## EFFECTIVE SOUL WORKERS ARE EQUIPPERS

A classic text dealing with the ministry of all the saints is found in Ephesians 4:11-12. The apostle Paul wrote, "And He personally gave some to be apostles, some prophets, some evangelists, some pastors and teachers, for the training of the saints in the work of ministry, to build up the body of Christ." The key word of the text is "equip." Those with ability and experience need to provide the saints with the resources required to encourage, admonish, and care for souls in pain. Soul-care leaders are coaches, enablers, and equippers for people in the body of Christ.

The word *equip* is important to congregational soul care. In his book *Liberating the Laity*, R. Paul Stevens gives the history and deeper meaning of this word as it relates to ministry: "Though *katartismos* (equipping or preparing) occurs in the New Testament only once (Ephesians 4:12), the word has an interesting history as a medical term in the classical Greek. A Greek doctor would 'equip' a body by putting a bone back into its correct relationship with the other members of the body. By reducing a fracture or realigning a dislocated limb, the doctor 'equipped' the patient. The task of an equipping soul-worker is to see that members of Christ's body who are in a broken relationship or are wrongfully connected to the body become correctly related."[1]

Stevens uses another analogy from Matthew 4:21: "The equipper is also like a fisherman mending his nets in preparation for another night's work. This is the literal use of the verb *katartizo*. James and John 'were in a boat with their father Zebedee, preparing [*katartizontas*] their nets' (Mathew 4:21). This literal use of the verb *katartizo* has the double meaning of undoing the harm and damage done by previous service and preparing the nets for further service."[2]

Stevens takes the concept of equipping further:

> Another meaning of *karatizo* is to create or to form. It suggests the image of a potter fashioning clay. In Romans 9:22, Paul speaks of objects prepared (*katerismena*) for destruction and compares these objects prepared for glory. ... After believers have experienced some suffering, God "will himself restore you [*katartisei*] and make you strong, firm and steadfast" (1 Peter 5:10).
>
> Equipping is building into people what they need to function effectively as servants of God in the church and in the world. This is God's work in which we have a share. And such molding by God takes place primarily when people are steeped in the Word of God "so that the man of God may be thoroughly equipped for every good work" (2 Timothy 3:17).[3]

Ministers and those with special training were given to the church to equip and prepare others to care for souls. Those soul workers can then, in turn, equip others. Difficulties, hurts, and suffering become the training ground for Christ followers to become more like Christ so they in turn can lead others.

NOTES

1. Paul R. Stevens, *Liberating the Laity: Equipping All the Saints for Ministry* (Downers Grove: InterVarsity, 1985), 111.
2. Ibid., 113.
3. Ibid., 117.

# CHAPTER 8

# TRAINING
# *Group*
# LEADERS

There should be a readiness, on our part, to investigate with candor to follow the truth wherever it may lead us.

—Simon Greenleaf

*Blessed be the God and Father of our Lord Jesus Christ, the Father of mercies and the God of all comfort. He comforts us in all our affliction, so that we may be able to comfort those who are in any kind of affliction, through the comfort we ourselves have received from God.*
—2 Corinthians 1:3-4

## Philosophy of Training

Many training paradigms are available for small-group leaders and topic-specific group materials. The training plan in this book emphasizes the communal and relational aspect of groups, not the logistics of how to present content. Content is critical, but the manner in which the content is delivered and processed determines a participant's ability to apply it to real life. Leaders have much more credibility if group members know and can experience the fact that they have been through a training process that requires the same level of authenticity and transparency that's expected of them.

Good group materials like those in the Picking Up the Pieces series provide adequate structure for leaders/facilitators within each of the topical books. These materials are concrete, even detailing how much time a specific group task should take with built-in flexibility to deal with issues that may require more attention. There's little need to train good leaders in the logistics of leading a group if you have the right materials. This training process identifies those who are ready to lead and those who need more time to become ready.

> *We intentionally focus on the heart and issues that could affect a leader's ability to relate deeply with people and build community.*

Some training methods focus too much on "doing" instead of "being." Doing puts too little focus on the heart of the leaders/facilitators. We intentionally focus on the heart and issues that could affect a leader's ability to relate deeply with people and build community.

## Purpose of Training

One vital aspect of training is to understand potential leaders' motivation to do the work of ministry. Psalm 51:6 instructs us, "Surely You desire integrity in the inner self, and You teach me wisdom deep within." God desires that we know truth in the core of our beings. When we're honest about our deepest motivation—not just what we say we believe but what our actions reveal—then we can know wisdom. Wisdom and love for God's people are essential elements for leadership. This kind of self-awareness cultivates authenticity in the group setting. Even though many of my trainees in the past have had a strong desire to lead or facilitate a group, as they progressed through the training process, they realized their motivation was not appropriate and they were not ready. In some training programs I've led, as many as 40 percent of those in the training came to realize or were told that they were not ready at that time in their lives to lead a group. We provide opportunities for those who need more time, healing, or growth to greet, direct, and dispense materials until they're ready to move into leadership. Many have been encouraged to attend one of the groups related to difficulties they have experienced.

> *We cannot lead people on a journey that we have not taken ourselves.*

**TRAINING MUST ALWAYS BE ABOUT REVEALING TRUTH TO THOSE SEEKING TO LEAD.** Whether the topic is grief, divorce, pornography, or postabortion trauma, teaching someone to follow a script over several weeks is not adequate in my experience. No leader should have his or her own agenda when leading a soul-care group. The training program in section 2 provides a process that's designed to reveal those who have their own agendas to fulfill.

One important trait for effective soul-care leaders is triumphant brokenness. The self-awareness process ensures that leaders operate from the perspective of understanding their own weaknesses and struggles so that they can extend to others the comfort they have received from God. God uses our suffering. Our words and actions to those in pain have little weight if we have not experienced suffering and God's comfort. Wounds in our own souls that have not yet been touched and redeemed by God can create unreasonable "fear of man," shame, relational issues, self-loathing, or other problems that can create obstacles for another's healing and restoration. We cannot lead people on a journey that we have not taken ourselves.

> *As the sufferings of Christ overflow to us, so our comfort overflows through Christ. If we are afflicted, it is for your comfort and salvation; if we are comforted, it is for your comfort, which is experienced in the endurance of the same sufferings that we suffer. And our hope for you is firm, because we know that as you share in the sufferings, so you share in the comfort.*
> —2 CORINTHIANS 1:5-7

> *As soul-care workers, our goal is to bring people face-to-face with themselves and, more importantly, face-to-face with God.*

**TRAINING MUST HELP LEADERS IDENTIFY WITH GOD'S INTERESTS IN OTHERS' LIVES.** When we identify with what God is doing in another person's life, we lose our own agenda, and the negative effects of our biases are minimized. We must not allow our own personal discomforts to get in the way of what God is doing. As soul-care workers, our goal is to bring people face-to-face with themselves and, more importantly, face-to-face with God. God's deep love for people must trump all my opinions, issues, and conditions. Leaders must learn to create an environment of love in which truth can be received. Authenticity from a leader breeds authenticity in a group. Without truth and transparency in a group, trust will be minimal, sharing will be superficial, and transformation will be only a fond hope. With truth, transparency, and trust, we invite the presence and power of God to be unleashed. Secrets and shame thwart soul care.

> There is no fear in love; instead, perfect love drives out fear, because fear involves punishment. So the one who fears has not reached perfection in love. We love because He first loved us.
> —1 John 4:18-19

## The Process of Training

Effective training will take several weeks. It will prepare you to lead topic-specific small groups. Leaders will also use forms and covenants during the training to ensure accountability and protect the church from liability.

In a leadership training group I conducted, one of the participants reminded us that she had dropped out of leadership training six months earlier. In her first training group, others became aware of her resentment toward her husband because of a betrayal. Accepting our feedback was difficult for her to accept. She was frustrated and felt misunderstood but agreed to attend a Picking Up the Pieces group using _Radical Reconciliation: The Journey of Forgiveness_. I also encouraged her to consider giving the training group a second chance when she felt ready. During the introductions in her second training group, her countenance and attitude change were remarkable. After addressing her personal issue through the soul-care process, she was excited and ready to lead the topic-specific group that would take others on the journey of forgiveness.

One of the first things we tell participants is, "Some of you won't make it." Be prepared to encourage those who realize early in the process that they are not yet ready to lead a group to stick with the training. This will likely help them in their healing journeys and, perhaps, enable them to be ready for the next round of leadership training.

The leadership training process is much like a counseling group. Often, participants know one another but are not accustomed to sharing on the level required in a soul-care group. You may also be uncomfortable at times, just like many of the people who will come to a group you lead. This is normal and necessary to build a sense of empathy among participants. Everything you learn in this experience should help you understand how to handle group members in the future. Strive for authenticity and transparency. A group leader will not foster either of these dynamics in their groups if they don't personally exhibit them.

> *Leadership training is designed to help future leaders learn more about themselves rather than provide a checklist for how to deal with specific situations.*

This process is difficult for some participants. It's designed to help future leaders learn more about themselves rather than provide a checklist for how to deal with specific situations. We do want to go over some specifics: how to deal with those who dominate, how to deal with those who become overly emotional, and how to identify those who need to be referred for more intensive care. In the end we want people to be leaders, not do leadership.

# GROUP
# LEADER
## *Training*
# PROGRAM

Training is everything. The peach was once a bitter almond; cauliflower is nothing but cabbage with a college education.

—MARK TWAIN, *Pudd'nhead Wilson*

# Administrative Guide

### Session 1
## Trust, Truth, Transparency—
## Foundation for Authentic
## Relationships

### Session 2
## Characteristics of
## a Group Facilitator

### Session 3
## Processing and Healing
## Personal Issues

*Reading 1: Wounded and Captive Hearts*

### Session 4
## Processing and Healing
## Personal Issues

*Reading 2: Breaking Strongholds and Living Free*

### Session 5
## Processing and Healing
## Personal Issues

### Session 6
## Group Processes
## and Forms

# Administrative Guide

Three words have been around ministry, counseling, and medical circles for many years. These words are important; they must be foundational in the heart of every soul worker willing to share others' pain and burdens. We must do the best we can with God's help to *do no harm.*

Group or individual soul work must always be done with humility and from a sense of our own brokenness, never from a sense of self-righteousness. Training is designed to ensure that all leaders have a healthy self-awareness and understand how their individual and relational brokenness might impact others. Training is a time to discover "integrity in the inner self" (Ps. 51:6) so that our motivation is to have no agenda or to allow unresolved personal issues to color our perceptions in a way that may harm others. Training will expose agendas and other issues that prevent people from identifying with God's interest in those who come to us in pain and confusion. Further, it is designed to promote authenticity and transparency and to help leaders develop trust among those who seek their help. Finally, training is designed to protect the church and its members by clearly establishing that we are about discipleship, ministry, and soul work and not amateur or professional counselors.

This training process is designed to focus on healing instead of harming, affirmation over advice, and love over legalism. We are all either agents for good or evil, and this process is about recognizing those things in ourselves that may harm others whether intended or not. Our commitment to the process of training correlates directly to our love for the Lord and for others. Our relationship with those in pain is more important than being right. The emphasis in these training sessions is on the *person* of the leader, not education, expertise, or previous training. The Great Commandment to "love your neighbor as yourself" is one of the most important criteria for a soul worker.

This training is not to equip people to lead specific groups but to be facilitators of healing. Trainers will discuss with church leaders which groups should be led by whom. Every training group includes people who do not know which group they should lead; and because of the structure of Picking Up the Pieces resources, they should be able to lead any group at the end of the training. If participants have specific life experiences related to topics, they may connect more quickly with members of the groups they lead, but such experience is not necessary. Some of the best leaders have not necessarily experienced trauma specific to the group they led. They simply created a safe place for hurting people to seek and find God in the midst of their confusion and conflict.

## Attendance and Rules

Since the training depends on each previous and successive week, to be considered for leadership, participants must attend all training sessions.

Circumstances may prevent consistent attendance in *some* situations. Communicate to potential participants that all participants considered for leadership should attend all training meetings. If someone cannot commit, he or she should let the leader know and plan to attend the next scheduled leadership training for Picking Up the Pieces studies.

## GROUP SIZE

Assuming about a 40 percent attrition rate (which reflects an average drop-out rate), the ideal starting size of a training group is 15-17 people. Attrition usually stops by the fourth week. Those who discover during the process of training that they are not prepared or ready to lead a group should be encouraged to stay in the training and serve in other ways. They can be greeters, sell books at tables set up in the group area, or assist group leaders. Usually, church leaders direct these people into a Picking Up the Pieces group that best fits the issues impacting them negatively and encourage them to go through training again at a later time. Communicate that church leaders want them to participate. Make sure they know they are valued even though the time is not right for them to lead.

## TRAINING PLAN OPTIONS

Training can effectively occur in one of three ways. Sessions 1 and 2 are primarily instructional; sessions 3-5 are primarily process oriented, and session 6 concludes the training process.

1. SIX WEEKLY TRAINING MEETINGS. The most effective way to conduct the training groups is weekly. The first two sessions have instructional elements while sessions 3-5 are more process oriented. Members training groups need child care, so picking a time when child care is available makes attendance easier for some members. Breaking the training into six weekly meetings provides participants an experience that is more consistent with the weekly groups they'll be leading.

2. ONE EXTENDED INSTRUCTION MEETING AND FOUR WEEKLY TRAINING MEETINGS. In some cases, and depending on the time of the year, it's more efficient to pick a block of time (at least three hours) on Saturday or Sunday to cover the first and second sessions. These two provide important instruction and lay the foundation for what is to come. You can then follow with four weekly meetings to complete the other sessions.

3. THREE EXTENDED TRAINING MEETINGS. Each meeting is three hours long. The first meeting is instructional, covering sessions 1 and 2. The second meeting should cover sessions 3 and 4, and the third meeting should cover sessions 5 and 6.

## WEEKLY ASSIGNMENTS

You'll find weekly assignments at the end of each session. Encourage participants to complete these assignments. While these assignments will help them process the content, you should not take time in the next session to deal with their homework except for the issues paper they write in preparation for presenting in sessions 3 and 4. If a member has a concern about the homework, deal with it quickly.

## LEADER HELPS

All boxed sections designated as "Leader Note" will have materials provided for the trainer. Teaching segments should take no more than 20 minutes to complete. The leader of this group establishes the tone by giving participants important information on the front end.

## BEFORE THE FIRST SESSION

The group purpose texts provide direction and the philosophical/theological underpinnings. Those going through the training are encouraged to complete these readings prior to coming to the first training session. You can use the Beatitudes to help potential leaders understand desired characteristics of group leaders. The assignments to read 1 John and James reinforce and establish a mind/heart-set for those desiring to participate.

Display sample copies of Picking Up the Pieces materials in the first session for participants to review quickly as they arrive so they will see that structure is provided within the materials. Often participants are a little anxious wondering if they will have the necessary structure and materials. Ensure trainees that the materials will provide the structure and how-to of group process. This helps them to be less self-conscious and less anxious about performance. Encourage them to focus on their own personal growth rather than on the groups they will lead. What they gain during these training sessions will lead to self-awareness, an essential foundation for group leadership.

Before the first session, assign participants to read James and 1 John.

# SESSION 1
# TRUST, TRUTH, TRANSPARENCY—
# FOUNDATION FOR AUTHENTIC
# RELATIONSHIPS

> LEADER NOTE: *Greet the group with warmth and share some personal background information (self-disclosure is what we are going to ask others to do shortly). Then share a brief description of the mission and vision for providing topic-specific groups. Include these points:*

- Reaching into the congregation.
- Reaching out into the community.
- Doing the work of ministry to assist pastor, staff, and Sunday School teachers.
- Equipping for a work God has called the church to do.

Follow the conversation about the mission and vision with a discussion about the importance of confidentiality. In addition to covering attendance, rules, mission and vision, and confidentially in the first session, you will also cover these topics:

- Trust, Truth, Transparency—Foundation for Authentic Relationships
- Biblical Forgiveness—What It Means and What It Doesn't Mean
- Confrontation the Right Way

## CONFIDENTIALITY
Information discussed in these groups is confidential (among group participants and facilitators). Information disclosed in the training group is not to be discussed with anyone outside the group. Group members are not to discuss any issues raised with anyone outside the group. Any breach of confidentiality will be dealt with openly within the group.

Confidentiality should only be broken under the following conditions:

- Any indication of harm to self or others
- Any indication of active abuse/harassment

These conditions require the member to notify the leader immediately. If the member finds other legitimate reasons, other than those listed above, for confidentiality to be broken, the following protocol is to be followed:

- Go to the member in question and discuss your concerns with him/her.
- Tell the member in question you feel his/her issue needs to come to the attention of the facilitator and why.
- Develop a plan (before ending the meeting) for communicating this information with the facilitator.

## THE THREE T's: TRUST, TRUTH, AND TRANSPARENCY

Good leaders are truthful, transparent, and trustworthy. Leaders don't pretend. They are real, the persons God made them to be. Facing problems truthfully is the only way to a healthy outcome. Leaders are to be authentic and truthful, and they cannot do this without relationship and community. God created people for relationship and not for isolation.

You cannot help others accept themselves as God made them to be if you hide behind a mask of competence or confidence. If you are dealing with insecure people, you must teach them authenticity by being transparent. Know when to challenge and when to support. Don't hesitate to disclose the hard times you have been through as you stand by those in their times of trouble.

To create a safe environment for sharing, growth, and healing in your group setting, you must be trustworthy. Members must trust your love for them if they are going to invite you along on their journey. They will not be transparent or truthful if they feel you are critical, judgmental, or that you will share their stories with others. Group leaders who are truthful and transparent about their own journeys engender the same quality in others. Remember the rule of the Three T's: No Trust without *Truth shared with Transparency*.

## APPLICATION FROM JAMES 4:7

*Submit to God. But resist the Devil, and he will flee from you.*
—JAMES 4:7

Here are three steps to submit yourself to God:
1. IDENTIFICATION. Examine your heart (thoughts and feelings). Take a few days to pray and list the specific thoughts, feelings, and behaviors that are inconsistent with God's will. Write them down.
2. CONFESSION. Seek God's forgiveness for those things revealed. You don't need publicly to confess specific details. It is more important to confess the particular sin associated with the acts. When the confession

is complete, engage in some ceremony to establish a specific event to challenge the Devil when he brings up shame and guilt.

3. OBEDIENCE. Follow God's plan to deal with each sin accordingly as you seek to maintain accountability in relationships affected by your wrongdoing.

Our hearts must be put right with God in order to move to the next step: "Resist the Devil and he will flee." We cannot resist a supernatural enemy without supernatural power. We cannot have God's supernatural power if we are not submitted and surrendered to Him. Resisting the devil is the natural outcome of a surrendered and submitted life. Resisting implies a stance. Resisting is a twofold process whereby if I want to stand against the devil, I prostrate before God (bow then stand).

As you engage in this process, the Devil will flee from your life. Submission is an ongoing and active process.

## EMOTIONS/FEELINGS

God gave us emotions for a reason. They serve a valuable purpose if they are kept in perspective. Here's an example.

When you have a fever, you know something is wrong in your body. You have an infection, and the fever is a symptom, letting you know to pay attention. You can take aspirin, and the fever will dissipate for a few hours. However, if you don't deal with the cause of the infection, the fever will return. Fever makes us feel bad; we ache, have chills, and are generally uncomfortable. Until we deal with the cause of the fever, our symptoms continue to worsen.

Emotions are like that. They are usually a symptom of some underlying problem that we have ignored or purposefully set aside. We can continue to ignore the emotions, distract ourselves, or hide the emotions without paying attention to the source of the problem. If we continue in this way, our symptoms will worsen.

Let's look at anger. Anger is almost always a secondary emotion. Usually anger comes on quickly and, for some of us, powerfully. Sometimes we realize that we get too angry over small things. We are not paying attention to our emotional fever.

If anger is a secondary emotion, what comes first? If we look carefully at ourselves, we begin to realize that feelings of hurt, fear, rejection, betrayal, and frustration usually come immediately before anger.

Contemporary and secular authors tell us that we should confront an offender with our anger and let him know how we feel. We are told that we have a right to be angry when we are treated in inappropriate ways. However, how often have you confronted someone with or in your anger and felt resolved and clean before God?

If anger is a response to a primary emotion, why not deal with the problem and not the symptom? We will learn how to deal with our anger before it turns into resentment and our resentment before it turns into bitterness.

Look at Ephesians 4:26-27: "Be angry and do not sin. Don't let the sun go down on your anger, and don't give the Devil an opportunity." When we do not deal with the cause of anger, this emotional fever can wreak havoc in our lives and the lives of those who love us. Do you have an emotional fever? Do you want to continue to take "an aspirin" now and then, or would you like to clean up the infection?

Paul gives an answer in Ephesians 4:31-32: "All bitterness, anger and wrath, insult and slander must be removed from you, along with all wickedness. And be kind and compassionate to one another, forgiving one another, just as God also forgave you in Christ.

> *Speaking the truth in love, we will in all things grow up into him who is the Head, that is, Christ. From him the whole body, joined and held together by every supporting ligament, grows and builds itself up in love, as each part does its work.*
> —EPHESIANS 4:15-16

## FORGIVE ONE ANOTHER

To forgive is to set a prisoner free and to discover that the prisoner was you.

—LEWIS B. SMEDES

> *Put on heartfelt compassion, kindness, humility, gentleness, and patience, accepting one another and forgiving one another if anyone has a complaint against another. Just as the Lord has forgiven you, so also you must forgive.*
> —COLOSSIANS 3:12-13

Read Matthew 18:21-35. When I forgive another, my appreciation of God's forgiveness of me deepens. We must first accept God's divine gift of grace and forgiveness before we can extend it to others. To choose not to forgive is to keep an event or injury alive which results in a life of self-imposed torture (Matt. 18:34). Unforgiveness allows the offender to have control of my spiritual, emotional, and physical well-being. How can I "pursue as my goal the prize promised by God's heavenly call in Christ Jesus" (Phil. 3:14) when I stay stuck in the past?

> *If you forgive people their wrongdoing, your heavenly Father*
> *will forgive you as well. But if you don't forgive people, your*
> *Father will not forgive your wrongdoing.*
>
> —MATTHEW 6:14-15

Unforgiveness prevents individuals from following through on many of the specifics of the Christian life and necessitates that they walk by the flesh and not by the Spirit. Our relationships offer us a spiritual training ground where we can develop holiness, and that includes the ability to forgive. Unforgiveness is a bondage that cripples marriages and relationships from their outset. It is a bondage that chokes out the abundant life Christ promised to those who would believe.

An unforgiving spirit is one of the most destructive forces in any relationship. Forgiving others is necessary if we are to receive God's forgiveness. When we are unforgiving, we transform our bodies from the temple of the Holy Spirit into a dungeon of anger, hate, and bitterness. If I hold people hostage through unforgiveness, I essentially prevent God from dealing with them and block my ability to have fellowship with God and with others. I must always pray that God will be as gracious to others as He has been to me. Unforgiveness prevents me from relying on God and is a direct contradiction to who God is.

- Forgiveness is an act of my will making use of God's grace in order to cancel a debt owed me. Forgiveness is a choice.
- Forgiveness is the purposeful removal of my desire to avenge or exhibit personal ill will toward someone who has hurt or injured me. God says that vengeance is His (Rom. 12:19).
- Forgiveness is freedom from the bondage of feelings that produce distress in my life and the lives of the ones who love me. Unforgiveness threatens my spiritual, emotional, and physical health. It is like an acid that destroys the container that holds it.
- Forgiveness is the settling of accounts (Matt. 18:23).
- Forgiveness is not approval of sin. It's not that you are saying the wrong is now right but that you are offering forgiveness anyway.
- Forgiveness is not restitution.
- Those who have hurt or injured you cannot undo what they have done. If you cancel a debt due to hurt or injury, you should not expect some type of payment from the one who hurt or injured you. If you forgive someone who owes you one hundred dollars, you have forgiven the debt and should not expect payment. This decision to forgive a debt cost you one hundred

dollars; forgiveness and freedom have a price. Jesus paid the ultimate price that we might receive God's forgiveness.

- Forgiveness is not necessarily reconciliation. Sometimes we have to forgive someone with whom we will not be reconciled (for example, deceased family members or those who remain in a sin state and threaten our spiritual, emotional, or physical well-being). We should, however, make every attempt to reconcile with those we forgive. Forgiveness is a choice you must make to open the door for reconciliation; but reconciliation is a process that takes two people, the injured and the offender.

- Forgiveness does not necessarily provide immediate trust. Trust and forgiveness are not the same. Trust is earned when the words and actions of the offender are consistent over time.

Prayerfully ask God to reveal to you persons whom you have not forgiven. This week spend time listing the names of your offenders and the offenses committed against you. When you feel the list is complete, copy the form below for each offender and carry it with you for a few weeks.

Lord, You have forgiven me for so much. You have extended Your forgiveness to me daily. Therefore, as an act of my will, and with Your help, I choose to forgive _____ (NAME) and cancel the debt of _____

_____ (GENERAL DESCRIPTION, BETRAYAL, REJECTION, ETC.). From this day forward with Your help, I renounce my desire to avenge the wrong committed against me and will show no more ill will toward the person(s) named above.

I realize the enemy will bring this offense to mind even after I have forgiven it. Since I am keeping this paper with me, I will take it out and reaffirm that forgiveness has been extended and cannot be taken back when memories or negative emotions flood over me. I will then pray wherever I am and thank You for extending Your forgiveness to me through Your Son Jesus Christ.

Signed: _____ (YOUR NAME)
Date: _____ (DATE)

# CONFRONTATION: RESOLVING CONFLICTS THE RIGHT WAY

When offering forgiveness, you will likely encounter a certain amount of confrontation. There are right and wrong ways to confront people. We hear a lot about confrontation in the world today. The world's model for conflict resolution suggests that when we have an issue with someone we are supposed to go to him and point out how he has wronged us. This model seldom works to the glory of God and does little to restore fellowship. Most of the time it raises a defensive attitude in the person being confronted.

According to Matthew 5:23-24, if your brother has something against you, you are to go to him and make it right before offering your sacrifice. Our response is: "Wait a minute! He is the one who wronged me!" However, if you are angry or resentful, your brother also has something against you. In order to stay clean before God, your job is to make the situation right whatever the circumstance. If you have broken fellowship with other believers, including your spouse, you have hindered fellowship with the Lord.

You'll find some basic differences between the natural method of confrontation and the supernatural. Think of it this way: My spouse said something that upset and hurt me a few days ago. I did not deal with it, and every time I see him or her, I feel resentment, and the fellowship between us has begun to deteriorate.

The world's model tells me I should confront my spouse and tell her what she did was wrong. Consider another approach. Imagine yourself going to your spouse and asking for a few minutes of her time. "Honey," you say, "I need to ask you to forgive me because I have harbored resentment the last few days. When you said _____, my feelings were hurt, and I began to let my feelings simmer and turn into resentment. Please forgive me."

You have pointed out no wrong in the other person. You have simply cleaned up your own temple, and any response you receive from the other person is between that person and the Holy Spirit. This is the supernatural method of conflict resolution. We get out of the way and allow God to work His way and His will in the situation.

You can never be an effective change agent without proper preparation. Are you holding on to any negative thoughts, motives, or attitudes about another such as self-righteousness, anger, bitterness, or condemnation.

If so, you are apt to turn a method of ministry into a means of destruction by personalizing, becoming adversarial, or confusing your opinion with God's will.

Confrontation is bringing truth to a place where change is needed.

> *You must not act unjustly when rendering judgment. Do not*
> *be partial to the poor or give preference to the rich; judge your*
> *neighbor fairly. You must not go about spreading slander among*
> *your people; you must not jeopardize your neighbor's life; I*
> *am the LORD. You must not hate your brother in your heart.*
> *Rebuke your neighbor directly, and you will not incur guilt*
> *because of him. Do not take revenge or bear a grudge against*
> *members of your community, but love your neighbor as yourself;*
> *I am the LORD.*
> —LEVITICUS 19:15-18

God intends confrontation to be an expression of our submission to Him in our relationships with others. Our failure to confront biblically is a form of idolatry. If we are afraid to confront, we either love something or our relationship with someone more than we love Him. We fear another's reaction more than His, or we love our understanding of peace more than His.

PRINCIPLE 1. To the degree that we give our love or hearts to something or someone else, we lose our ability to confront. If we love God above all else, confrontation is an extension and expression of that love.
The quality of our love for our brothers and sisters is a reliable indicator of our love for God. When we don't confront, we don't serve God but allow others to continue in sin so that we can stay comfortable.
A rebuke (confrontation) free of unrighteous anger is a sign of biblical love. Many of us have distorted truth and have learned above all to be nice. But the Bible repudiates covering sin with silence. How can we let those we love deceive themselves with excuses, blame, and rationalizations? How can we watch them get more enslaved by the fleeting pleasure of sin?
PRINCIPLE 2. The depth of love in a relationship can be judged by the degree of honesty that exists. Truth telling in love should be a normal part of healthy Christian relationships.

PRINCIPLE 3. Confrontation keeps you from sharing in the other person's guilt. To refuse to rebuke or confront is to be a moral accomplice in another's sin. As you think about this, view your unwillingness to confront as rebellion. How does this feel?

PRINCIPLE 4. God ordained rebuke to restrain sin. We are either part of His work, or we stand in His way.

PRINCIPLE 5. Confrontation does not force another to deal with you; it places him before the Lord. When another is in the presence of God, he is moved to conviction. Conviction moves the other toward confession. Confession initiates repentance, and repentance results in restoration.

> *The instruction of the LORD is perfect,*
>   *reviving the soul; the testimony of the LORD is trustworthy,*
>   *making the inexperienced wise. . . . Who perceives his*
> *unintentional sins?*
>   *Cleanse me from my hidden faults. Moreover, keep Your servant*
> *from willful sins; do not let them rule over me. Then I will be*
> *innocent,*
>   *and cleansed from blatant rebellion. May the words of my mouth*
>   *and the meditation of my heart*
> *be acceptable to You, LORD, my rock and my Redeemer.*
>                                         —PSALM 19:7,12-14

LEADER NOTE: *Allow all group members to share their call into this type of ministry. It is always good to hear from those who have struggled with specific issues (addictions, loss, grief, etc.) and feel burdened to help others. Many participants will stray from the directions and get into conversation not related to the request. Here is where trainers demonstrate the principles of group leadership. This is the 2 Corinthians 1:3-7 dynamic you desire. Keep the time limits; reinforce time limits prior to beginning this section of the group.*

*Let the group know that some of them may not make it to the end of the six weeks of training. Share this with the group multiple times. Always communicate this with love and grace. Some people just are not ready to lead a group. State that being a group leader is only one aspect of the ministry.*

# SESSION 1 ASSIGNMENTS

**CONFIDENTIALITY.** Your trainer has gone over the importance of confidentiality. Write in the space provided how you would respond if asked by a friend or staff member at your church how a certain person in your group was progressing.

Does the thought of this kind of question or interaction make you uncomfortable?

If so, how?

**THE THREE T's.** The three T's of healthy community are detailed earlier in this session. Prayerfully consider each of these characteristics and rate yourself on each one. Use a scale of 1 to 5, with 1 representing work needed on this characteristic and 5 representing strength in this area.

_____ Truthful

_____ Transparent

_____ Trustworthy

**FORGIVENESS.** As you review the material on forgiveness, identify how it has changed your previous understanding of biblical forgiveness. Are there people in your life that you haven't forgiven? How willing and ready are you to do so now? Follow the instructions in "Forgive One Another."

**CONFRONTATION.** As you process and read through the concept of biblical confrontation, what are some of your personal sticking points? Based on this concept of confrontation, what have you learned about yourself?

**READING.** Read chapters 1, 2, 3 of this book before the next session.

# Session 2
# Characteristics of
# a Group Facilitator

LEADER NOTE: *Most pastors and church leaders know church members pretty well. Look for people with these characteristics. The training process will help you identify anyone who is not yet ready to lead a group.*

## Group Leadership Qualities

The key characteristics in selecting potential leaders for soul care are humility, honesty, hunger, and grace.

HUMILITY. People who demonstrate humility are aware of their own brokenness and manifest this in their relationships with a servant's heart.

HONESTY. These people don't make excuses; they take responsibility for their actions and don't blame others for their bad choices.

HUNGER. People who hunger for God's Word and apply its truths in their lives are good candidates for leading Picking Up the Pieces groups.

GRACE. Good leaders know the power of grace because they have received it. Their stories give evidence of the experience of difficulties and a dependence on God and others for help. These may be people who have experienced one or more of the difficulties represented in the Picking Up the Pieces materials.

Good leaders are confident in their lack of confidence. They don't have to have all the answers and seldom give advice even when asked. They are not harsh, judgmental, or legalistic when they are treated unfairly. They are relational and supportive. They are kind and have compassion.

LEADER NOTE: *Overview the following content in session 2. This content was the heart of chapter 7, Selecting the Right Leaders.*

## Characteristics of Effective Soul-Care Workers

Christian leaders fully accept that their positions are gifts from God and their influence is dependent on His help. When problems are overwhelming and there are no easy answers, leaders call on God for help and ask for wisdom. They also teach others how to bring problems before the Lord.

LEADERS ARE AUTHENTIC AND SERVE GOD'S AGENDA, NOT THEIR OWN. They genuinely believe God's leadership principles are not true because they work; rather, they work because they are true. In Psalm 26:1-4 David invited God to examine him, to test his integrity. This is a statement of authenticity. Authenticity is a primary requirement for soul workers.

> May integrity and uprightness keep me,
> for I wait for You. . . .
> Vindicate me, LORD,
> because I have lived with integrity
> and have trusted in the LORD without wavering.
> Test me, LORD, and try me;
> examine my heart and mind.
> For Your faithful love is before my eyes,
> and I live by Your truth.
> I do not sit with the worthless
> or associate with hypocrites.
>
> —PSALM 25:21; 26:1-4

LEADERS COUNT THE COST (LUKE 14:28-35). Serving as a soul worker is expensive. It will cost time that would be easier spent elsewhere. Leaders use their time and words carefully. When we have influence over others' lives, the responsibility is overwhelming. The longer we remain in leadership, the greater the personal responsibility.

LEADERS ARE TRUTHFUL, TRANSPARENT, AND TRUSTWORTHY. Leaders don't pretend. They are real, the persons God made them to be. Facing problems truthfully is the only way to a healthy outcome. Leaders are to be authentic and truthful, and they cannot do this without relationship and community. God created people for relationship and not for isolation.

You cannot help others accept themselves as God made them to be if you hide behind a mask of competence or confidence. If you are dealing with insecure people, you must teach them authenticity by being transparent. Know when to challenge and when to support. Don't hesitate to disclose the hard times you have been through as you stand by those in their times of trouble.

To create a safe environment for sharing, growth, and healing in your group setting, you must be trustworthy. Members must trust your love for them if they are going to invite you along on their journey. They will not be transparent or truthful if they feel you are critical, judgmental, or that you will share their stories with others. Group leaders who are truthful and transparent about their own journeys engender the same quality in others. Remember the rule of the Three T's: *No Trust without Truth shared with Transparency.*

LEADERS ARE RELATIONAL. Leaders recognize the importance of building relationships. If soul-care leaders don't enjoy developing relationships with people, something is wrong. When soul workers feel people are a nuisance, life is out of sync.

LEADERS ARE SERVANTS. Authentic Christian leaders seek neither the spotlight nor the corner but seek only the place God wants them to be. True humility is not passive; humble soul workers recognize their total dependence on God and their highly valuable contribution. Leadership is a gift of service. When leaders don't know what to do, they do what needs to be done. Look for people who have a track record of service.

## CHARACTERISTICS OF EFFECTIVE SOUL-CARE WORKERS

The hearts of effective soul workers resonate with Psalm 19:7,12-14: "The instruction of the LORD is perfect, reviving the soul; the testimony of the LORD is trustworthy, making the inexperienced wise. . . .Who perceives his unintentional sins? Cleanse me from my hidden faults. Moreover, keep Your servant from willful sins; do not let them rule over me. Then I will be innocent, and cleansed from blatant rebellion. May the words of my mouth and the meditation of my heart be acceptable to You, LORD, my rock and my Redeemer."

Grace and humility are two concepts I've highlighted throughout this book. Effective soul-care practitioners help others out of an awareness of their personal brokenness. It's critical for all soul-care workers to approach their work with meekness that comes from an awareness of God's grace in their own lives. Otherwise, they may come across harsh and legalistic; they will do more harm than good in the life of the one seeking help.

SOUL-CARE WORKERS MUST BE HUMBLE. Nothing in God's kingdom is stronger than humility or weaker than pride. We must always remember that anything begun in self-confidence ends in shame. Humility always overcomes evil with good. There is no good apart from Christ, yet prideful leaders continue in self-willed directions no matter the cost to His bride. Pride, a need to control, arrogance, and anger will draw us to condemn others. Jesus gave His life to wipe out shame and condemnation.

SOUL-CARE WORKERS MUST BE SELF-AWARE. Accurate self-awareness is essential for a soul-care worker. Defensiveness and self-protection have no place in the arena of soul care. A soul-care worker helps people release the shame and condemnation Jesus removed from us.

SOUL-CARE WORKERS MUST UNDERSTAND THE DYNAMICS OF PAIN. When we're injured, our Christian principles often disappear. Satan works with cunning, speaking and repeating lies to keep us captive and ineffective.

He works in the realms of fear, selfishness, and divisiveness. He loves to draw us back into the darkness of shame and condemnation, pointing to our sins, failures, and weaknesses with an accusing finger.

SOUL-CARE WORKERS MUST BE KNOWLEDGEABLE AND TRUTHFUL ABOUT THE POWER OF SIN. Each person involved in the ministry of soul care must come to the knowledge that, while we are new creations in Christ, we continue to fight for freedom against the Devil and the sin that dwells in us. The apostle Paul addressed these issues in Romans 7:13-25 and Galatians 5:16-26. Believers today deal with the same struggles as did believers in the early church.

SOUL-CARE WORKERS MUST BE FAMILIAR WITH GOD'S WORD AND APPLY IT TO THEIR LIVES. Paul told Timothy and Titus to appoint leaders in the church who exhibited Christlike character (1 Tim. 3:1-13; Titus 1:5-9). Soul-care workers must be aware of the issues in their own lives as revealed by the Holy Spirit through the Word of God.

SOUL-CARE WORKERS DO NOT DISTORT THE CHARACTER OR AGENDA OF GOD. God is holy, just, righteous, merciful, long-suffering, and full of grace. We must be careful that we do not use our personal dispositions to justify a distortion of any of God's characteristics. The primary responsibility of anyone called into the ministry of soul care is to identify with God's interests in the lives of those who need help; we must align with God's agenda in the lives of others. Frankly, this is a struggle for everyone called into this challenging ministry. We are to maintain transparency and truth within the community of our fellow soul workers. We must maintain a passionate and authentic relationship with God. We must constantly and consistently ask the Holy Spirit to search our hearts and apply the "law of the Lord" to our own lives. We must allow Him constantly to restore our souls if we are to be effective in leading others to healing and transformation.

# SESSION 2 ASSIGNMENTS

CHARACTERISTICS OF A GROUP FACILITATOR. Review the characteristics of a group facilitator. Rate yourself honestly on each one. Use a scale of 1 to 5, with 1 representing "work needed" on this characteristic and 5 representing strength in this area.

_____ Humility

_____ Honesty

_____ Hunger

_____ Grace

> LEADER NOTE: *Divide participants into two groups. Group 1 will turn in papers and present their issues in session 3; group 2 will turn in papers and present their issues in session 4. Each person will have no more than five minutes to present the issue in the session. Now is a good time to be encouraging and reassuring. Let participants know that they will be experiencing the same types of feelings that participants in their groups will be experiencing in the future.*
>
> *Sharing in a group setting will be difficult for some participants. Let them know that while you understand the difficulty they are facing, the paper and sharing in the group are essential elements of the training. These experiences are at the heart of the training and are not optional for anyone who wants to complete the training and lead a topic-specific small group.*

WRITING. Write a one-page paper about the issue you will share with the group during one of the next two sessions. The issue should be a real, personal issue (written in first person about your own experience or feelings)— resentment, conflict, anger, etc.—typed or handwritten on one page. Be prepared to discuss the same issue with the group for five minutes or less. People in group 1 will bring their papers for session 3, prepared to share the same experience. People in group 2 will bring their papers for session 4, prepared to share the same experience.

READING. Read chapters 7 and 8 of this book before the next session.

# Session 3
# Processing and Healing Personal Issues

The process of sharing and listening gives participants opportunities to experience what members of topic-specific small-groups experience. When these people lead their own groups, they will know more about the range of emotions people in their groups are feeling because they have participated in a group where they listened and shared their own issues.

The experience of sharing your own woundedness and hearing others share their stories prepares you to relate to those in a group you will lead. How you as a leader respond in leading a group to process their stories will either move a group ahead or hinder the group you lead.

## Sharing and Listening

Sharing members will learn from the process what it is like to share personal information with a group. Listening members will learn to process their own experiences as they hear others share about their own lives.

After members tell their stories, the group will process how hearing others' stories affects those who hear.

- Can you relate?
- What is your comfort level when you hear other people's painful stories?
- Do you feel critical?
- Do you feel sympathetic?

Members react in different ways. Discerning how you feel and hearing others express their reactions will help you prepare to hear such stories when you lead topic-specific small groups. Sharing members can also talk aloud about their experience of voicing personal stories and how they are processing their feelings of vulnerability, fears, and other emotions.

- Does the sharing seem authentic or minimized?
- Do you feel relief or regret for having told your story?

After each sharing member finishes, the leader will ask listeners or other sharers if they would like to respond. Some will give advice, others will quote Scripture, and some will talk about how they hurt along with the presenter. At the end of the sharing member's time, the leader will process with the sharing members how the different feedback felt to them. This is a great learning opportunity since they will all better understand how group participants experience different styles of feedback.

- Did you feel encouraged and supported?
- Did you feel criticized?
- Did you feel that others were preaching at or to you?
- Did you feel loved and affirmed?

Participants may respond with surprise at hearing about issues they never knew others had experienced, or they may respond with surprise at another's willingness to reveal the intimate details of their lives. When you lead a group, you will be better prepared to receive such stories from hurting people.

This is also an opportunity to learn about giving and receiving feedback. The goal of the listener is not to be judgmental or to preach to those sharing their lives. The purpose is not to give advice. The goal of a small-group leader is to facilitate the process, not condemn or judge. People who do this may see that they will need to change how they process information.

- How do you feel about the entire process of sharing and listening?
- How do you perceive the level of authenticity, grace, or support experienced?
- What was it like for sharing members to receive feedback?

# SESSION 3 ASSIGNMENT

AVENUES TO A HEART'S CAPTIVITY. Read the material that follows session 3. Spend some time reflecting on how the areas explained might interact with your story. Ask the question for your heart and the question to God listed at the end of the reading. Record what you hear.

# READING 1
# WOUNDED AND CAPTIVE HEARTS

## SEEING THROUGH THE LENS OF THE LARGER STORY

Proverbs 4:23 tells the critical importance of guarding our hearts: "Guard your heart above all else, for it is the source of life." As our physical hearts pump life to the parts of our bodies, our spiritual hearts are wellsprings of life to all that we are and all that we do. God has written His story on our hearts, God is focused on our hearts, and our own personal stories find their home there. When our hearts are wounded or bound, all of life is affected.

> *[God] has made everything appropriate in its time. He has also put eternity in their hearts, but man cannot discover the work God has done from beginning to end.*
>
> —ECCLESIASTES 3:11

Whenever we deal with issues or pain in our lives, we need to be aware of how our stories intersect with the larger story, the story God has written on our hearts. Our world did not just happen as a series of random events. We did not just appear in this world by accident as a blip on the earth's time line. We know there's a greater, unseen reality. "The Larger Story into which we all were born is the greater, unseen reality that God reveals through Scripture and His Holy Spirit. This story includes perfect harmony and closeness dispelled by a failed insurrection . . . the deadly fight between destroyer and redeemer . . . paradise lost . . . a beauty to be rescued . . . the daring rescue under the cover of night . . . ongoing dangerous battles . . . final banishment of evil . . . and the ultimate restoration of paradise."[1]

Biblical truth is set within the context of this larger backstory in the spiritual realm. Unlike humanistic approaches that ignore God, we need to understand our life journeys in the context of the larger story, God's story and the cosmic clash between good and evil. "The Larger Story goes beyond our specific journeys; it goes beyond our individual lives in this world; it even goes beyond the collective lives of humanity that span the centuries. The Larger Story began before life on earth. It's the story we were all born into and exist for. Without it our lives are only a meaningless series of joyful and painful events followed by death."[2] Here's the basic story:

ACT 1, INSURRECTION IN PARADISE. Before the creation of man, God created a paradise in the heavenlies, but evil was born in the heart of one of His most wonderful creations. Satan launched a rebellion in heaven, inciting other angels to join him in an attack against the Creator. God halted the insurrection and cast out Satan and one-third of the heavenly hosts.

ACT 2, MAN'S CREATED GLORY AND FALL. In the beginning of our world, God created us uniquely in His own image and without sin (Gen. 1:27). This was something God's enemy could not bear, so in his cunning he deceived Eve, and Adam disobeyed God (Gen. 3). This choice brought sin into our world and our hearts—spoiling paradise, our intimacy with God, and our original glory.

> *The Father . . . has enabled you to share in the saints' inheritance*
> *in the light. He has rescued us from the domain of darkness and*
> *transferred us into the kingdom of the Son He loves, in whom we*
> *have redemption, the forgiveness of sins.*
> —COLOSSIANS 1:12-14

ACT 3, JESUS RESCUED AND REDEEMED US. Through Jesus' death and resurrection, He has already conquered evil and sin once and for all; their fate of destruction is sealed. However, Act 3 is not the end of the story. Although all who accept Jesus' sacrifice for themselves will be saved, we still have to live in this fallen world. Author and professor Eric Johnson explains living in the paradox of Act 3: "The old is already over but still in us. The new is yet to come but has already begun."

> *We do not give up; even though our outer person is being destroyed,*
> *our inner person is being renewed day by day. For our momentary*
> *light affliction is producing for us an absolutely incomparable*
> *weight of glory. So we do not focus on what is seen, but on what is*
> *unseen; for what is seen is temporary, but what is unseen is eternal.*
> —2 CORINTHIANS 4:16-18

ACT 4, OUR RESTORATION AND REDEMPTION FULLY REALIZED. Paradise will be restored and sin eradicated forever. The redemption of our lives will be complete. We will be restored to the original glory that God had planned for us from the beginning. The great wedding feast will inaugurate an eternity of deeper and deeper intimacy with our Creator in paradise restored.

> *Be sober! Be on the alert! Your adversary the Devil is prowling*
> *around like a roaring lion, looking for anyone he can devour.*
> —1 PETER 5:8

# THE PROBLEM OF SUFFERING

Entire books have been written on the problem of suffering, and the following list is in no way a complete answer to that problem. However, it helps a great deal, as we process our issues and pain in order to find healing, to consider why bad things happen:

1. There's a real villain in the story that the Bible calls "the ruler of this world."
2. He uses lies and makes us question God's goodness.
3. He uses live ammunition, and his attacks are real.
4. His goal is to cause us to doubt the heart of God toward us.
5. The world system is blinded and corrupt, with people seeking their own way rather than God's.
6. Even though each of us as Christ followers becomes a "new creation" (2 Cor. 5:17) and God has given us good and noble hearts, we still carry around the "flesh"—our set of distorted desires, our old patterns of behavior, our false beliefs, and the sin that still lives in us (Rom. 7:20).
7. God longs for our freedom and for an intimate relationship with each of us. God allows freedom of choice, even bad or evil choices, because without freedom, true mutual love and relationship are not possible.

> *I know that nothing good lives in me, that is, in my flesh. For the desire to do what is good is with me, but there is no ability to do it. For I do not do the good that I want to do, but I practice the evil that I do not want to do. Now if I do what I do not want, I am no longer the one doing it, but it is the sin that lives in me.*
> —ROMANS 7:18-20

# HOW OUR HEARTS BECOME CAPTIVE

Even though God has already sealed Satan's fate through Jesus' death and resurrection, Satan is still "prowling around" (1 Pet. 5:8) and using his primary tactics of deception and accusation to take us out. He wants to make us believe that God is not good, to put his twisted perspective on every event, to wreak pain and havoc in our lives, and ultimately to destroy us. Satan and his demonic forces want to keep us out of the glory that we were intended to live in and the intimacy that God wants us to share with Him and others. With our flesh and sin still living in us, we can easily fall for these schemes.

We all experience pain in our lives at times, and there are many ways for us to escape or avoid the pain. The enemy strategically shoots arrows or uses the wounds in our lives to distort our identity, our perception of who we are. He continually whispers lies and accusations about who we are, who God is, God's heart toward us, and the intimacy God wants us to share with Him. Author Ron

Keck has developed the following model to illustrate the process of our hearts' being captured and enslaved. Although we are all different, common threads are evident in people's struggles and hopes for healing.

## Captive Heart Model

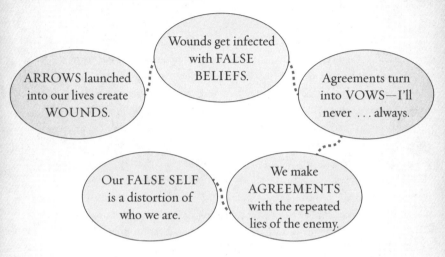

*Captive Heart Model & Critical Path to Healing developed by Ron Keck*

This model is intended to assist you in becoming aware of unhealthy dynamics in your life that may seem "normal" to you. We can become accustomed to certain ways of thinking and relating to others, knowing on some level that things just aren't working; yet we are unable to make real change. On our part change basically requires awareness and action; it also requires the presence and power of God. This model provides a concrete way for you and others to begin the process of awareness.

Spend some time working through the five components openly and honestly. Begin by acknowledging that wounds cause pain and that in pain we often find coping strategies. Let me give you an example. If you were barefooted and someone dropped a heavy rock on your foot (whether intentional or accidental), bones would break, and you would experience immediate and long-term pain. You would limp, adjusting the ways you think and act. If you ignored the pain and did not seek help as you walked through life, you would have to compensate with your other foot, leg, and muscles. If you compensate long enough, your walk might become a well-worn and comfortable style that feels normal to you.

Let's extend this example into the emotional and spiritual realm. Whether intentional or accidental, when we have been wounded, we hurt, we limp through relationships, we compensate, and eventually the ways we walk through life may begin to feel normal. Wounds hurt, and coping mechanisms may be the only way we can get through certain times in our lives, but unhealthy thinking and behavior can hurt us and others. We don't have to blame or make excuses for the ways we've had to compensate, but we cannot heal if we don't acknowledge wounds and the distorted beliefs and behaviors they can create. Pain in our lives can alter our perceptions of God, ourselves, and others. In times of pain, our enemy often launches accusations and lies about who we are, who God is, and what our world is like. As we rehearse those lies over and over, we will come to agree with them and accept them as truth.

Let me take this one more step. What happens when someone close to you happens to step on your broken foot? Your immediate reaction is to jump back and push the person away, protecting yourself from experiencing pain again. You've learned something. You may vow to yourself, "I'm going to keep my distance and never let someone hurt me like that again." Can you see the analogy? We do the same thing emotionally. Even though people are not responsible for the wound, they remind us it's there and resurface the pain. We don't like pain, and so we do whatever we can to escape or avoid it. Our false beliefs are reinforced in situations like these. Even if what we believe deep inside is false, we will act on those beliefs as if they are true. We may even make unhealthy vows to ourselves or live with a protective mask to cover what's really going on inside to avoid the pain.

To find healing and real transformation, we need to acknowledge past wounds and ask God to help us identify false beliefs that we've accepted as true—not our surface beliefs but what we really believe in the depths of our souls. We need to recognize our methods of self-protection and the unhealthy thought and behavior patterns we've adopted. This example and model are simply ways to increase your awareness and help you address these areas with God within your supportive community. Honesty is the beginning and freedom the end result, but we must be willing to stay in our pain long enough to find that freedom.

## WOUNDS

Strategic arrows are launched into our lives to create wounds: a difficult loss, painful circumstances, a traumatic event, neglect, abuse

**LIES**

Our wounds become infected with lies or false beliefs: "God has abandoned me too." "I'm a failure." "Nobody cares; it's up to me to look out for me."

**AGREEMENTS**

Satan repeats lies until we make agreements to accept them as truth: "I'm on my own now." "There's no hope." I can't live without it." "This is all I deserve."

**VOWS**

Once agreements are made, vows are soon to follow: "I will never again . . ." "From now on, I will always . . ."

**FALSE SELF**

False agreements and vows feed the false self: Our distorted views about who we are. The masks we wear to cover our true selves. The greater the distance between our false self and who we truly are in Christ, the greater the personal destruction and dysfunction we experience.

This model is not necessarily linear. Our stories and our identities can be distorted through any of the five points in many different situations. We will likely have to battle in one or more of the following areas to experience God's healing and restoration:

- Identify and renounce the lies that we've embraced.
- Break the agreements we've made with false beliefs and replace them with truth.

- Renounce the vows we've made and replace old vows with new ones.
- Refuse to live out of our false self and embrace who we really are in Christ.
- Remember that self-protection isolates us and that we were created for relationship.

# QUESTIONS FOR REFLECTION

In which area(s) of life do you feel the greatest amount of struggle? Use the illustration above and identify some of the "rocks" and the "wounds" in your life. With God's help, list some lies or false beliefs that have hurt you or protected you in the past.

Does this Captive Heart Model shed any light on your current struggles or situation? Can you see ways in which the enemy has exploited your story? Write about it.

Spend some quiet time alone with God. Ask, "God, please help me see ways that my heart has become captive? What lies or vows are dragging me down?" When you ask God a question, expect His Spirit to respond to your heart and spirit. Be careful not to rush or manufacture an answer. Don't write down what you think the "right answer" is. Don't turn the Bible into a reference book or spiritual encyclopedia. Just pose your question to God and wait for Him to speak personally in a fresh way. Anything God speaks to your heart will always be consistent with Scripture.

NOTES

1. Ron Keck, *Colossians: Embrace the Mystery* (Nashville: Serendipity by LifeWay, 2008), 5.
2. Ron Keck, et.al., *Redeeming the Tears* (Nashville: Serendipity by LifeWay, 2005), 47.

# SESSION 4
# PROCESSING AND HEALING PERSONAL ISSUES

> LEADER NOTE: *All members in group 2 will turn in their papers.*
> *Check to see that all group 2 participants have written a paper.*
> *Note quickly the topic of each. After the session return all the papers.*

The process during this session is the same as session 3, with sharing and listening roles reversed for the two small groups. Listening members from session 3 turn in papers on experiences and issues.

The experiences of sharing and listening enable participants opportunities to understand what members of topic-specific small-groups experience and to connect with them more quickly. When these people lead their own groups, they will know more about the range of emotions people in their groups are feeling because they have participated in a group where they listened and shared their own issues.

The experience of sharing your own woundedness and hearing others share their stories prepares you to relate to those in a group you will lead. How you as a leader respond in leading a group to process their stories will either move a group ahead or hinder the group you lead.

## SHARING AND LISTENING
Sharing members will learn from the process what it is like to share personal information with a group. Listening members will learn to process their own experiences as they hear others share about their own lives.

After members tell their stories, the group will process how hearing others' stories affects those who hear.
- Can you relate?
- What is your comfort level when you hear other people's painful stories?
- Do you feel critical?
- Do you feel sympathetic?

Members react in different ways. Discerning how you feel and hearing others express their reactions will help you prepare to hear such stories when you lead topic-specific small groups. Sharing members can also talk aloud about their experience of voicing personal stories and how they are processing their feelings of vulnerability, fears, and other emotions.

- Does the sharing seem authentic or minimized?
- Do you feel relief or regret for having told your story?

After each sharing member finishes, the leader will ask listeners or other sharers if they would like to respond. Some will give advice, others will quote Scripture, and some will talk about how they hurt along with the presenter. At the end of the sharing member's time, the leader will process with the sharing members how the different feedback felt to them. This is a great learning opportunity since they will all better understand how group participants experience different styles of feedback.

- Did you feel encouraged and supported?
- Did you feel criticized?
- Did you feel that others were preaching at or to you?
- Did you feel loved and affirmed?

Participants may respond with surprise at hearing about issues they never knew others had experienced, or they may respond with surprise at another's willingness to reveal the intimate details of their lives. When you lead a group, you will be better prepared to receive such stories from hurting people.

This is also an opportunity to learn about giving and receiving feedback. The goal of the listener is not to be judgmental or to preach to those sharing their lives. The purpose is not to give advice. The goal of a small-group leader is to facilitate the process, not condemn or judge. People who do this may see that they will need to change how they process information.

- How do you feel about the entire process of sharing and listening?
- How do you perceive the level of authenticity, grace, or support experienced in the group?
- What was it like for sharing members to receive feedback?

---

LEADER NOTE: *Spend this time assisting those who are struggling with the issues they have shared. The facilitator should work to move the group in a healthy direction. Don't allow one person to dominate. Be attentive to draw all participants into the discussion.*

---

# SESSION 4 ASSIGNMENT
## BREAKING STRONGHOLDS AND NEW CREATION.

Read the material that follows session 4. Spend some time reflecting on how the truths revealed might affect your story. Ask the question for your heart and the question to God listed at the end of the reading. Record what you hear.

# READING 2
# BREAKING STRONGHOLDS
# AND LIVING FREE

Somehow we've come to accept the idea that non-Christians live in bondage and Christ followers live in freedom. We may not actually say to someone that he shouldn't have issues in his life if he's following Jesus, but in subtle ways we can demonstrate that we don't expect, and certainly don't want to deal with, areas of bondage in our lives or the lives of others.

## DIVINELY POWERFUL WEAPONS

Reading 1: "Wounded and Captive Hearts" provided the context of the larger story for understanding the fierce spiritual battle for our hearts and souls. If we want to see real change, two keys are required: *awareness and action*, both guided by the presence and power of God. The focus of the Captive Heart Model in reading 1 was primarily *awareness* of unhealthy, harmful, or sinful dynamics. As God begins to reveal to us our wounds, false beliefs, vows, and false selves, it's time to take action with the divinely powerful weapons God has put at our disposal.

> *Although we are walking in the flesh, we do not wage war in*
> *a fleshly way, since the weapons of our warfare are not fleshly,*
> *but are powerful through God for the demolition of strongholds.*
> —2 CORINTHIANS 10:3-4

Scripture often tells us to walk by the Spirit and not to walk according to our flesh. Yet so many of us try again and again to battle in our own self-efforts, using the same old techniques of stuffing desires, working harder at self-control, and looking for strict accountability. While these aren't necessarily bad, these are what Paul refers to in 2 Corinthians 10:3 as weapons of the flesh. If all we achieve in soul care is helping people to keep the lid on their sins and the bandages covering their wounds, then we do no lasting good. We need to acknowledge that the battle we must engage in is spiritual. As we learn to pick up divinely powerful weapons, we can help others do the same. Many divinely powerful weapons and resources are identified through the teaching and stories of Scripture; let's focus on a few that are foundational.

*We have access to divinely powerful weapons and resources.*

# DEADLY HEART BLOCKAGES

After emphasizing that our battle is spiritual, Paul explains in 2 Corinthians 10:4-5 that we have access to spiritual weapons, which are "powerful through God for the demolition of strongholds." Paul goes on to explain about destroying these fortresses or strongholds: "We demolish arguments and every high-minded thing that is raised up against the knowledge of God, taking every thought captive to the obedience of Christ." Imagine an ancient fortified castle with its massive fortresses or strongholds. Pushing with all your strength on the castle with your shoulder is a pretty ridiculous attack. Now imagine the kind of siege it would have taken to destroy a stronghold like that. You would need an army and some powerful weapons. In the same way the spiritual battle in soul care requires a sustained assault on the strongholds in our lives. The word *destroy* in the Greek refers to the act of violently casting down or obliterating the strongholds in our lives.

Another analogy that helps illustrate the strongholds we must destroy is a physical heart blockage. According to CardiologyChannel.com, "in most cases, blockage occurs as a result of coronary heart disease, also called atherosclerosis, a condition in which plaque (deposits of cholesterol and fatty material) build up in the arteries and partially or completely block blood flow. When the surface of a plaque tears or ruptures, a blood clot (thrombus) can form and completely block the flow of blood in the artery."[1]

Spiritual strongholds are like the buildup in our arteries. The larger the blockage, the more it impedes proper function of our hearts. In order for the life-giving blood to flow properly in and out of the heart, the blockage must first be removed. In the same way we need to remove the blockages to our spiritual hearts so that healing and healthy living can occur. As in cardiac treatment, the first step is to determine where the blockage is. Then we can focus on removing it.

Notice the sequence of the assault plan in 2 Corinthians 10:4-5. Too often we try to reverse the sequence. We cannot take captives until we tear down the fortress, and we cannot restore the proper flow of blood until a heart blockage is removed. We need to identify and demolish our spiritual strongholds, and then we can begin to take every thought captive and make it obedient to Christ. When we engage an enemy thought, we need to grab it, tie it down, and interrogate. Then, after we learn all we can from that captive thought, we can't keep giving it other chances to sabotage us.

*We demolish arguments and every high-minded thing that is raised up against the knowledge of God, taking every thought captive to the obedience of Christ.*

—2 CORINTHIANS 10:4-5

# THE BASIC WEAPONS

Throughout this book three basic spiritual resources are highlighted:

- Brutal honesty—truth, trust, and transparency
- Courageous community
- Intensive prayer

Secrets and silence are the soil for shame and condemnation. In a caring community built on truth, trust, and transparency, shame is washed away by truth and godly love. In Ephesians 5:8-11, Paul directs, "For you were once darkness, but now you are light in the Lord. Walk as children of light—for the fruit of the light results in all goodness, righteousness, and truth—discerning what is pleasing to the Lord. Don't participate in the fruitless works of darkness, but instead, expose them." The goal in soul care is not judgment and condemnation but loving accountability as together in Christ we overcome the "fruitless works of darkness."

Ephesians 4:25 shows the interrelation of two of these basics: "Speak the truth, each one to his neighbor, because we are members of one another." James 5:16 shows the power in linking all three: "Confess your sins to one another and pray for one another, so that you may be healed. The intense prayer of the righteous is very powerful." When we care about someone deeply and we know well his struggles, then we can pray for him with heartfelt intensity and power. Author and counselor Larry Crabb explains how togetherness in Christ encourages movement toward Christ like that described in Ephesians 4:11-14, "Connecting begins when we enter the battle for someone's soul. It continues as we prayerfully envision what Christ would look like in that person's life. It climaxes when something wonderful and good pours out of us to touch the heart of another."[2]

> *Connecting begins when we enter the battle for someone's soul.*
> *He personally gave some to be apostles, some prophets, some*
> *evangelists, some pastors and teachers, for the training of the*
> *saints in the work of ministry, to build up the body of Christ,*
> *until we all reach unity in the faith and in the knowledge of God's*
> *Son, growing into a mature man with a stature measured by*
> *Christ's fullness. Then we will no longer be little children, tossed*
> *by the waves and blown around by every wind of teaching, by*
> *human cunning with cleverness in the techniques of deceit.*
> —EPHESIANS 4:11-14

# Engaging in the Kingdom Reality

Typically we view the Bible, the Spirit, and community as tools or weapons to use rather than as living things with the power to transform us. Kyle Strobel in *Metamorpha* explains, "The kingdom is a place where wisdom reigns, where justice and righteousness prevail, and yet it is brought about by the Spirit and not by seeking those things for our own ends. Our mistake has always been to try to *make the kingdom happen* on our own instead of engaging in the kingdom reality."[3] Hebrews 4 highlights the necessity of hearing from God and entering into His rest and care. The words and presence of God offer life and piercing power.

> *The word of God is living and effective and sharper than any*
> *two-edged sword, penetrating as far as to divide soul, spirit, joints,*
> *and marrow; it is a judge of the ideas and thoughts of the heart.*
> —Hebrews 4:12

Jesus makes clear in Matthew 16:18 that the gates of hell will not prevail over His power, which He's given to the church.

> *You are Peter, and on this rock I will build My church, and the*
> *forces of Hades will not overpower it. I will give you the keys*
> *of the kingdom of heaven, and whatever you bind on earth is*
> *already bound in heaven, and whatever you loose on earth is*
> *already loosed in heaven.*
> —Matthew 16:18-19

Because we don't live in the kingdom reality, or even think about it most of the time, we don't pick up the keys to the kingdom that we've been given. What could happen if we made use of these keys and began to bind and loose things in the spiritual realm with all the resurrection power of Jesus, the great I Am?

We need individually and collectively to explore the adventure of being in Christ and living with Christ in us—not in eternity but here and now. Colossians 1:27 and 3:3 explain the mystery wonder of our union with God in Christ. "God wanted to make known to those among the Gentiles the glorious wealth of this mystery, which is Christ in you, the hope of glory" (Col. 1:27). "You have died, and your life is hidden with the Messiah in God" (Col 3:3).

# Renouncing and Replacing Lies

We will likely have to battle in one or more of the following areas to experience God's healing and restoration:

- Identify and renounce the lies we've embraced.
- Break agreements we've made with false beliefs and replace them with truth.
- Renounce the vows we've made and replace old vows with new ones.
- Refuse to live out of our false self and embrace who we really are in Christ.
- Remember that self-protection isolates us and we were created for relationship with one another and with God.

To find healing and real transformation, we need to acknowledge past wounds and ask God to help us identify false beliefs we've accepted as true—not our surface beliefs but what we really believe in the depths of our souls. King David wrote Psalm 51 after having an illicit affair with Bathsheba, having her husband killed, and then taking her as his wife. In this powerful psalm David models for us a life of truth, transparency, and trust before God. Like David we must learn to open our hearts to God, to allow Him to pour truth into our innermost beings, to walk with Him through the brokenness and pain of our lives (even valleys of shadows), to embrace His cleansing, to plead for His presence, to engage life in His power, and to allow Him to restore our joy and gladness! David was far from perfect, but he chose the road few dare to travel.

> *Surely You desire integrity in the inner self, and You teach me wisdom. . . . Let me hear joy and gladness; let the bones You have crushed rejoice. . . . Create a clean heart for me and renew a steadfast spirit within me. Do not banish me from Your presence or take Your Holy Spirit from me. Restore the joy of Your salvation to me, and give me a willing spirit.*
>
> —Psalm 51:6,8,10-12

# Ongoing "Old Man" and "New Man" Tension[4]

Part of knowing truth in the innermost being requires increased honest dialogue from head to heart, recognizing that parts of the heart are not yet fully under God's redemptive influence. This dialogue must be honest, experiential, and lived out in community. The goal of our soul's journey is to diminish the influence of the "old man" and proportionally increase the influence of the "new man" in our beliefs, life experiences, and relationships.

*You took off your former way of life, the old man that is*
*corrupted by deceitful desires; you are being renewed in the spirit*
*of your minds; you put on the new man, the one created according*
*to God's likeness in righteousness and purity of the truth.*
—EPHESIANS 4:22-24

The first step to the process of living as a new creation in Christ is to view the "old man" or "the flesh" as an appendage—a thing, an object that is not who we really are. We must stop identifying with the "old man" and continue to live as the "new man" that we have become in Christ. The more we consent to and delight in God and our new identity in Christ, the more we access divinely powerful resources, which in turn help undermine the control and influence of the flesh in our lives.

> Far removed from perfection, we must move steadily forward, and though entangled in vices, daily fight against them.
>
> —JOHN CALVIN

The newness of life—to be eternally alive—is to be relational, God centered, and communal. We focus our minds, hearts, and lives on the triune God. These same new life realities must be lived out among other believers to further develop our lives. In a special way the encouragement and challenge we offer to our Christian brothers and sisters help open our souls to new kingdom realities.

My real self is who God declares me to be in Christ, seated with Him in the heavenly places. The great challenge for Christ followers is to believe that they are who God says they are despite the "old man" they still drag around. The "old man" is characterized by resistance to God and promotion of self. Our redemptive stories ebb and flow, but we make progress only as we stay in the battle for ourselves and for one another. As we develop contempt for the Devil, the worldly system, and our old, unhealthy ways of relating to people and to God, we deepen our separation with the "old man" and live increasingly in the "new man" and in newness of life.

# QUESTIONS FOR REFLECTION

As you look at the area(s) of life in which you struggle most, what blockages or strongholds do you think might be the root cause? Ask God to reveal the stronghold(s) you most need to demolish now.

What secrets and shame in your life need to be exposed to the light of truth and glory of grace? What lies or vows do you need to renounce and replace with truth?

Which divinely powerful weapons and resources are strongly at work in your life? Which are currently lacking? Why do you think these things are lacking?

Spend some quiet time alone with God. Read aloud David's prayer from Psalm 51. Ask God, "How do You feel about the failures and the losses in my life?" Then ask, "How do You feel about me when I fail?" When you ask God a question, expect His Spirit to respond to your heart and spirit. Don't rush or manufacture an answer. Don't write down what you think the "right answer" is. Don't turn the Bible into a reference book or spiritual encyclopedia. Just pose your question to God and wait for Him to speak personally in a fresh way. Anything God speaks to your heart will always be consistent with Scripture.

## NOTES

1. *www.cardiologychannel.com/heartattack/index.shtml*, accessed December 7, 2008.
2. Larry Crabb, *Connecting* (Nashville: Thomas Nelson, 2004), 170.
3. Kyle Strobel, *Metamorpha* (Grand Rapids: Baker Books, 2007), 174.
4. The concepts for the old man-new man tension were provided by Eric L. Johnson and used by permission.

# Session 5
# Processing and Healing
# Personal Issues

> LEADER NOTE: *Review and process all training to date. Discuss*
> *dynamics and how the group dealt with difficult issues. Discuss with*
> *the group those who do not feel ready to lead. Discuss difficult situations*
> *with those who dominated or consistently went over time limits. Use*
> *these issues as training opportunities to help participants prepare to*
> *lead their Picking Up the Pieces groups.*

Review your personal experiences and recall the community of leaders and relationships that have developed through the training process. What have you learned that you can apply to your own leadership style in working with topic-specific small groups? For example, what did you learn as you observed the leader as he or she dealt with members who went too long? Note things you learned that will impact the way you lead a group in the future.

## A Fresh Theology of Caring

If you want to see the full level of transformation that God wants to bring into the hearts of your people, you'll need to consider a practical theology of caring. A number of constructs and concepts have been incorporated within the Picking Up the Pieces approach and resources. Many of the paradigms listed in this chapter have been adapted from Serendipity's strategic vision work.

## Leading Transformational Journeys

1. Caring is at the heart of soul care. Formulas, checklists, and heavy-handed techniques don't heal; they harm. Soul care is conducted by broken people for broken people.
2. The goal of soul care is not to teach people propositional truth but to lead people on experiential and transformational journeys.
3. Jesus' model for spiritual transformation included approaches such as creating events, leveraging the power of story, doing life together, using the senses, movement and activity learning, modeling, creating tension or paradox, and provocative questions.
4. Healing, freedom, and transformation best occur within the context of community (Jas. 5:16). Community needs to be an ongoing part of any soul-care dynamic.

5. God is not a formula to be mastered but a mystery to be embraced. All too often we operate from an unrecognized need to control God or keep Him within some framework. We memorize promises, create formulas, and sometimes even misread Scripture to avoid taking a journey into the unknown of trusting God; and yet that's what this life is all about. Faith is about embracing the mystery of God and His gospel.

6. The gospel is much bigger than we tend to allow; we often don't embrace its fullness. For too long we've focused only on the gospel of conversion (and it is good news), but Jesus seemed to highlight the gospel of the kingdom. The gospel is incomplete without a kingdom focus.

7. Our modern era is overly goal directed, pursuing a destination mentality. While goals and destination are important, perhaps the postmodern era has rebalanced us more toward a journey mentality.

8. The Bible is the ultimate authority and truth source; it alone is our sole authority in matters of faith and godliness. However, revelation and illumination aren't bound to any one method.

9. There is no doubt from Scripture that we are all born in sin, totally depraved, unable to save ourselves, and in need of a Savior. We are image bearers that reflect a distorted image of our Creator because of sin. These distortions in us and in our fallen world result in pain and suffering. There's only one solution: living out the new life we are promised in Christ. In the context of a redemptive community, we can help one another grasp the hope of this new life, and we can help identify and correct distortions so we continue to reflect an increasingly truer image of our Creator.

10. Sin is not something we can manage. Sin affects every aspect of our being. The reality of sin permeates every aspect of our being and our world. There are no prescriptive hoops we can jump through, no behavior we can manage, and no work we can perform to escape the certainty of our condition. There is only one cure, a growing and deepening relationship with the Christ who came to set us free.

11. We often overlook a vital part of the redemption story. Why do we always hear teaching on the doctrine of original sin and subsequent depravity and seldom, if ever, about the doctrine of original glory? We cannot appreciate the depths of the fall until we acknowledge the glory originally bestowed and eternally promised. Neither can we appreciate the restoration that's coming or the substance of redemption/regeneration that occurs at conversion apart from this understanding.

12. We should view our lives through the lens of the larger story (God's story and the epic struggle between good and evil). As we do this, we begin to see truth about God's heart, ourselves, our stories, and the world in which we live.

13. Discipleship doesn't equal behavior modification or sin management. Discipleship is spiritual transformation.

14. Honesty, truth in the deepest places, is another vital key to healing and transformation. This is God's desire and prescription for us. We must be willing to risk taking our deepest questions to God and wait for Him to speak into our stories personally and specifically.

15. God allows us to make choices! Galatians 5:1 indicates that Christ set us free for the sake of freedom alone. God is fully sovereign, and yet His sovereignty does not negate certain freedoms.

16. Redemptive Bible study emphasizes breaking strongholds, healing, grace, and redemption rather than focusing on behaving consistently with a rigid set of standards.

17. The fight to be free doesn't really end. Healing and freedom most often require a journey. Christ followers must fight for freedom and be willing to embark on a journey into healing.

18. In community we realize that we are broken people. The enemy of our soul wants us to dwell on such things to the point of self-loathing, self-pity, and eventually self-destruction. God desires to transform destructive thoughts and emotions into a constructive relationship with Him and others.

19. We need God's truth to set us free. When people are hurting and captive, what heals them and sets them free is not a list of truth statements but God's personal assurance that He is present, He is powerful, and He loves them more than they can possibly imagine.

Soul care is not a program or tidy formula; it's messy. There really are no easy answers or biblical one-liners; these only tend to further alienate those consumed with guilt, shame, and feelings of inadequacy. Soul care is a lifelong journey, and all of us want someone to recognize, in the midst of our mistakes and failures, that our hearts are good, that someone really cares. We want to forgive and be forgiven. We want to know and be known. We want to be loved.

> LEADER NOTE: *Introduce your church's concept and vision for soul-care ministry. If this is the first group involved in this training, introduce the concept and model for Picking Up the Pieces soul-care ministry found in chapters 4, 5, and 6.*

# SESSION 5 ASSIGNMENT

READING. Read chapters 4, 5, 6 of this book before the next session.

# SESSION 6
# GROUP PROCESSES AND FORMS

LEADER NOTE: *Be prepared to review all of the forms in section 3 and to explain their importance. Make copies of forms 4, 5, and 10 in section 3 of this book for all members. Have members sign forms, assign groups to new leaders, provide materials, and choose participants (those not yet ready to lead) to help in ancillary areas.*

Welcome participants to the final session. Review all of the forms in section 3. Distribute copies of forms 4, 5, and 10 for members to sign. The church should retain a copy of each member's signed Soul-Care Leadership Pledge (form 4) and Leadership Training Group Covenant Form (form 5) to keep on record. (This will take approximately half of the allotted training time.)

Thank trainees for their participation. Allow time for trainees to share how the training has impacted them and changed their lives.

Close with prayer. Pray for those who will lead small groups in studies using *Picking Up the Pieces* resources. Pray for participants in future groups. Pray for the church's soul-care ministry.

# FORMS
## *for Developing and Implementing*
# YOUR SOUL-CARE MINISTRY

Everything must be done decently and in order.

—1 Corinthians 14:40

FORM 1
# VISION AND MISSION DEVELOPMENT FORM

FORM 2
# SOUL-CARE PLANNING TEMPLATE

FORM 3
# LEADERSHIP ASSESSMENT FORM

FORM 4
# SOUL-CARE LEADERSHIP PLEDGE

FORM 5
# LEADERSHIP TRAINING
# GROUP COVENANT FORM

FORM 6
# PASTORAL COUNSELING LOG

FORM 7
# PROFESSIONAL COUNSELOR
# TOP 10 QUESTIONS

FORM 8
# WHEN TO SEEK HELP

FORM 9
# RECOMMENDATION FOR
# PROFESSIONAL CARE

FORM 10
# SOUL-CARE REGISTRATION
# AND CONSENT FORM

# VISION AND MISSION DEVELOPMENT FORM

## JESUS' MISSION
"The Spirit of the Lord GOD is on Me, because the LORD has anointed Me to *bring good news* to the poor. He has sent Me to *heal the brokenhearted*, to *proclaim liberty* to the captives, and freedom to the prisoners; to proclaim the year of the Lord's favor, and the day of our God's vengeance; to *comfort* all who mourn, to *provide* for those who mourn in Zion; to give them a crown of beauty instead of ashes, festive oil instead of mourning, and splendid clothes instead of despair. And they will be called righteous trees, planted by the LORD, to glorify Him" (Isa. 61:1-3, emphasis added).

## OUR CHURCH'S MISSION (KEY PURPOSES)
1.
2.
3.
4.
5.

## OUR SOUL-CARE MINISTRY'S MISSION (KEY PURPOSES)
1.
2.
3.
4.
5.

## OUR SOUL-CARE MINISTRY'S VISION (WHERE WE SEE OUR CHURCH IN 3-5 YEARS)
1. A concise, compelling picture of the future

2. Far-reaching but attainable

# Soul-Care Planning Template

## Short-Term Focus and Detailed Action Plans (1-2 Years)
*List action plans in each category with projected dates for completion.*

Prevention—*incorporating soul care in ongoing church ministries*

Intervention—*launching targeted soul-care ministries and topic-specific groups*

Intercession—*developing your prayer warriors*

Pastoral Counseling—*adjusting your current approach as needed*

Professional Counseling—*creating the best scenario for your church members*

## Long-Term Focus and General Action Plans (3-5 Years)
*List action plans in each category with projected dates for completion.*

Prevention—*incorporating soul care in ongoing church ministries*

Intervention—*launching targeted soul-care ministries and topic-specific groups*

Intercession—*developing your prayer warriors*

Pastoral Counseling—*adjusting your current approach as needed*

Professional Counseling—*creating the best scenario for your church members*

# LEADERSHIP ASSESSMENT FORM

Selecting group leaders is one of the most important considerations in creating a successful soul-care ministry. Use this form to select potential leaders for the training process. The training process is designed to identify and deselect those who are not ready to lead a group at this time.

Name of Potential Leader: _____

Date: _____

| Quality | Needs Improvement | | | | Very Strong |
|---|---|---|---|---|---|
| **HUMBLE/SERVANT** | I | 2 | 3 | 4 | 5 |
| *Notes:* | | | | | |
| **HONEST/TRUTHFUL** | I | 2 | 3 | 4 | 5 |
| *Notes:* | | | | | |
| **HUNGRY FOR GOD** | I | 2 | 3 | 4 | 5 |
| *Notes:* | | | | | |
| **TRANSPARENT/AUTHENTIC** | I | 2 | 3 | 4 | 5 |
| *Notes:* | | | | | |
| **GRACE-FILLED/COMPASSIONATE** | I | 2 | 3 | 4 | 5 |
| *Notes:* | | | | | |
| **RELATIONAL/SUPPORTIVE** | I | 2 | 3 | 4 | 5 |
| *Notes:* | | | | | |
| **COMMITTED/TRUSTWORTHY** | I | 2 | 3 | 4 | 5 |
| *Notes:* | | | | | |

# SOUL-CARE LEADERSHIP PLEDGE

Church or Ministry Name: _____

Believing that the privilege of leading people to a knowledge of God's Word and an uncompromising commitment to Christian discipleship is worthy of my service, I covenant as a soul-care worker to the following:

## BELIEF AND DOCTRINE

1. I believe and will teach that the Bible is the divine, inspired Word of God, without error in its original form (2 Tim. 3:16).
2. I will practice the spiritual disciplines in my life that align with the Bible and doctrines held by this church.
3. I will cooperate with the established church leaders and organizational life of this church with regard to the curriculum materials and program plans.

## CONDUCT

1. I will order my conduct to be consistent with the principles of the New Testament and seek leadership and strength from the Holy Spirit. I agree to be an example of Christian living so that my conduct may not cause anyone to stumble and that I may be faithful and efficient in my work (Rom. 15:1-2; 1 Cor. 8:9-13; Eph. 4:1).
2. I will contribute God's tithe to the Lord through the budget of my church (Mal. 3:10; 1 Cor. 16:2).
3. I will endeavor to make sharing the gospel a part of my life (Prov. 11:30; 2 Cor. 2:14-16).
4. I will pray regularly for the participants of this ministry, the church, staff, and elected leaders (Ex. 7:11-13).
5. I will support the church vision and structures as led by the pastor and church leaders (Heb. 13:16-18).

## RESPONSIBILITY

1. I will be regular and punctual in attendance, and in case of unavoidable absence, I will give notice as far in advance as possible (1 Cor. 4:2; 1 Tim. 3:1-5).
2. I will make thorough preparation for the lesson and for my other duties (2 Tim. 2:15).

3. I will take advantage of opportunities for leadership training, studies in group methods, and development of my Christian life so that I may be well informed about good leadership principles and methods (Prov. 15:28b; 2 Tim. 3:14-15).
4. I will be loyal to the church, striving to attend worship services (Heb. 10:25).
5. I will seek to discover and meet the needs of those who are enrolled as members or prospects (Rom. 15:1-7; Gal. 6:2).

If at any time I am unable or unwilling to fulfill this covenant in all good conscience, I will relinquish my position of leadership as a soul-care worker. If at any time church leaders advise me to relinquish my position of leadership, I will do so willingly and promptly.

Print Name: _____

Signed: _____

Date: _____

# LEADERSHIP TRAINING GROUP COVENANT FORM

Before reading and signing this form, please read and sign the Leadership Pledge (form 4). It is important for this training group to covenant together. You'll be asking your groups to covenant together in this same way using similar group covenants provided in the Picking Up the Pieces studies. It's also important that you support one another as group leaders since individually you will be supporting the members of your group.

**PRIORITY:** All training sessions are integrated, with each session building on the previous ones. While I am in this group, I will give it priority, and I understand that if I miss a training meeting, I will not be able to lead a group.

**PARTICIPATION AND FAIRNESS:** I have a responsibility to the training group and its members. I commit to participation, interaction, and honest disclosure and feedback. I will avoid dominating group discussions and sharing times. I will be fair and kind to others and stay within the time frames given by the trainer.

**HOMEWORK:** The homework experiences are integral and vital to the training process so I commit to completing the assignments given me.

**RESPECT AND OWNERSHIP:** I agree to extend grace in all my discussions, feedback, and sharing. I agree to avoid hurtful criticisms, recognizing that this will impair others' motivation to be truthful. If I notice that I'm feeling critical or resentful, I agree to share my feelings, owning them and taking responsibility for them. Offensive language is not permitted.

**CONFIDENTIALITY:** The trainer has clearly communicated what confidentiality is, and I agree to have all questions answered before leaving the first training session. Anything said in these training sessions, stays here. NO EXCEPTIONS. This is vital to creating an environment of trust, truth, and transparency.

**CARE AND SUPPORT:** I give permission to others in this training group to contact me. I make myself available to be part of a support network of trainees as long as I am involved in this ministry.

**ACCOUNTABILITY AND INTEGRITY:** I agree to let members of this training group hold me accountable to commitments I make. I agree to build relationships with other trainees, understanding that group leaders share a common concern for those in the groups both now and in the future. I also understand that my role is not about giving advice, whether solicited or not. During this process and while leading soul-care groups, I agree to avoid the use of mood-altering chemicals (prescription drugs are clearly permitted).

**EXPECTATIONS OF FACILITATORS:** The discipleship I will be doing (individual or group) is not professional counseling or therapy. I am a volunteer who feels called into this soul-care ministry.

I agree to all of the above: _____

Date: _____

# PASTORAL COUNSELING LOG

Name of Counselee: _____

Date: _____

Name of Pastor or Minister: _____

## REASON(S) COUNSELING WAS INITIATED

## SPIRITUAL PROBLEMS OR ISSUES DISCUSSED

## MINISTERIAL GUIDANCE GIVEN (Biblical Principles, Text Supporting Guidance)

## NEXT STEP(S) SUGGESTED

Note: Church or ministry records can at times be subpoenaed by the court.

# PROFESSIONAL COUNSELOR
## TOP 10 QUESTIONS

It's prudent and necessary to ask professionals a few questions if you are going to refer members of your congregation to them. Meeting with professionals face-to-face is always a good idea when you're seeking the best for your people.

## IN GENERAL, LOOK FOR SOMEONE WHO:
- can provide evidence of solid biblical and counseling training/experience.
- loves people, perseveres through difficult situations, and is confident that Jesus works in His people.
- believes the Bible is inerrant and foundational for giving wisdom and direction.
- gives clear evidence of a personal, passionate relationship with Jesus Christ.

## TOP 10 QUESTIONS TO ASK
1. Will you share your personal testimony with me?



2. Tell me about your training (school, seminary, and licensure) and experience.



3. What theoretical approach do you use in your counseling? Please describe your process.



4. Tell me about your view of the critical path to healing.



5. Where do you go to church, and what is your involvement?



6. Tell me about your family.

7. How do you approach counseling when one member of a marriage wants a divorce?

8. Do you use the Bible and prayer in your sessions? If so, how do you use them?

9. What are your fees, and what provisions do you make for people with limited resources?

10. If we referred people to you, how could we assist you in your counseling? *Note: All licensed professionals must have a counselee sign a Release of Information to discuss any aspect of the counseling relationship with a referral source. If the counselor does not acknowledge this even if answering all of the other questions to your satisfaction, you should be concerned.*

While this is not an exhaustive list, answers to these questions will give you plenty of information to determine whether you're comfortable referring to this person.

## CREATING A REFERRAL LIST

Professionals have areas of expertise. Specializations include marriage and family, individuals, children, depression, addictions, and so forth. One counselor will *not* be able to meet all of the needs of your church members so you will probably need to create a list of specialties with names and contact information for each counselor. Always inform those you refer that you have interviewed the professional counselors but that they, as the people who need to be comfortable in counseling, have the ultimate decision-making responsibility. Engage in personal contact with all professionals on your list, even if they are recommended by someone you've already interviewed and with whom you feel comfortable.

Both AACC (*www.aacc.net*) and Focus on the Family (*www.focusonthefamily.com*) maintain extensive lists of Christ-centered professional counselors.

# When to Seek Help
*Situations That Require Immediate Action*

Having to seek the help of your pastor or church leaders for a group member should never be viewed as failure on your part. Our motto is, "Do no harm." If you ever sense someone needs immediate help, get it! Being in over your head should never be personalized but viewed as proactively seeking the best for those you serve in your ministry.

## Thoughts of Self-Harm
- A person might have had, or is having, recurring thoughts about wanting to die. These thoughts might be something like: "My family would be better off if I were dead," or, "Sometimes I just want to drive into a tree."
- Important: Anytime a person has a plan for self-harm, you should take immediate action. A plan might sound like this: "I keep thinking about the loaded gun I have in my closet," or, "I've been thinking about taking the pills in my medicine cabinet."

## Thoughts of Harming Others
- An individual who continues to have thoughts about harming or killing someone could present a danger.
- Important: Anytime a person has a plan for harming someone, you should take immediate action.

## Self-Destructive Behavior
- Anytime an individual harms himself or herself (such as cutting self or burning self), seek help.
- You should also seek help if you notice signs of not eating (anorexia) or bingeing and purging (bulimia).

## Thoughts That Indicate Their Reality Is Different from Yours
- Some people may actually be out of touch with reality. An individual can be suspicious, even paranoid (thinking a family member is trying to poison him or her for example).
- When thoughts present without any basis in reality, professionals call this "delusional activity." Spiritual oppression might also be possible. Anytime someone indicates hearing voices or seeing things that aren't there, seek help.

## Medical Conditions
- Some medical conditions affect emotional and spiritual health. A medical doctor should immediately deal with any condition related to endocrine or hormonal systems that a person reports as interfering with his or her ability to participate in soul care. A medical doctor should evaluate and approve the person for participation if a medical condition is worsened by the stress of participation.
- Many times the people in your group will be on various medications. You should communicate with leaders about the effect of the medications on their ability to participate. If someone has a significant medical condition, a medical doctor should be apprised of the person's involvement in soul care and give his or her approval for continued participation.

## Depression and Anxiety
- Depression and anxiety are pervasive in our culture today. If a group member is experiencing undiagnosed or untreated clinical depression, anxiety, or other emotional problems, progress will be minimal or nonexistent.
- Following are symptoms of depression. If any three of them are reported or obviously displayed, the person should be referred to a medical doctor or a competent clinician immediately.
    1. Suicidal thoughts (see above)
    2. Inability to enjoy activities that used to be pleasurable
    3. Sense of hopelessness or helplessness
    4. Social withdrawal
    5. Sudden and significant weight gain or loss
    6. Loss of concentration or impaired memory
    7. Insomnia (difficulty falling asleep, waking up in the middle of the night, or early morning awakening)
    8. Alcohol or drug abuse
    9. Frequent crying or tearfulness over minor issues
- Following are observable symptoms of anxiety.
    1. Panic attacks
    2. Obsessive thinking, sometimes with compulsive behaviors
    3. Heart racing, sweaty palms, cold hands, or other physical discomfort
    4. Very nervous around others
    5. Difficulty speaking or interacting

*Note: these lists are not exhaustive but provide enough information for you to identify group members who might need additional assistance with depression or anxiety.*

# LACK OF PROGRESS

- If a person has been coming to your group for some time and there's minimal or no progress, this person may need more intensive care. If an individual is disruptive, dominating, or does not complete assignments, this is often an indication that he or she is not ready to get better. This person may need additional help.
- A person in this condition may impair your group's progress. Do not hesitate to discuss these issues with your church staff or pastor.

If you identify any of these key points in people who attend your group, seek help from your pastor or someone in ministry leadership. The person you contact depends on the size and structure of your church. Make sure you know the name and contact information for this person before you ever start your group. You can be certain that, if you're involved in this ministry for any length of time, you will need help.

FORM 9

# RECOMMENDATION FOR PROFESSIONAL CARE

_____ Church, Soul-Care Ministry

This confirms that I met Pastor _____
on (date) _____ _____.

On the basis of information I disclosed in our meeting, Pastor _____
and I determined that my current situation/needs fall outside the scope of
ministry (*refer to the signed Registration and Consent Form*) and that I need immediate
professional care.

I acknowledge that I have been referred for professional assessment/treatment
and confirm that I intend to follow this recommendation.

Signature: _____
Date: _____

Witness: _____
Date: _____
*My signature above indicates my agreement to follow the recommendation.*

_____

I acknowledge that I have been referred for professional assessment/treatment
and confirm that I am unwilling to follow this recommendation.

Signature: _____
Date: _____

Witness: _____
Date: _____
*My signature above indicates my refusal to follow the recommendation.*

If I have refused to follow Pastor _____'s
recommendations for professional assistance, I agree to assume full responsibility
for my well-being and agree to release and hold harmless _____
_____ Church, the staff of _____
_____ Church, or any of its agents.

# Soul-Care Registration
# and Consent Form

This form is to be read and signed by anyone interested in joining a soul-care group or intending to participate in the leadership training program prior to participating.

## Information

This information is being provided so that you will understand the conditions for participating in our soul-care ministry. Please read this carefully and ask questions about anything that seems unclear. Your signature indicates your understanding and acceptance of these conditions. Our intention is to clarify the purpose of this ministry and to help all participants have clear expectations.

## Type of Ministry

Soul-care ministry provides insight from the Bible and Christian materials. All care and instruction provided serve a ministry function. Our purpose is facilitating hope, healing, and the deepening of your relationship with the Lord and others. Soul-care ministries may involve individual discipleship, topic-specific groups, pastoral counseling, or other small groups. These are ministries of the church and *not* professional services.

## Not Professional Advice

Although our volunteers may work in professional fields outside the church setting, when serving in our soul-care ministry, they are providing biblically based instruction and their role is ministerial; they do *not* serve in a professional capacity when leading soul-care venues.

## Confidentiality

Confidentiality is an important aspect of soul care. The soul-care ministry will protect information as confidential. In several situations, however, you may need to share information with others:

1. To seek advice from another staff/minister/volunteer in this church or ministry about how to address a particular problem
2. To comply with any and all applicable state and/or federal laws, such as those dealing with abuse
3. To prevent harm to the participant or someone else
4. To inform soul-care leaders because they need to know the situation
5. To advise/consult a pastor for any of these reasons when the person attends another church

## Records/Information

I understand that I am involved in a Christian ministry and receiving care for my soul. I understand that the person providing individual or group soul care is providing a ministry function and I am not involved in a professional relationship with him or her. I agree that I will under no circumstance have soul-care staff or volunteer or his or her notes/records subpoenaed for any past or future legal proceedings.

## Resolution of Difficulties

On rare occasions a conflict may develop between an individual and people providing soul care. In order to make sure any such conflicts will be resolved in a biblically faithful manner, we require all individuals to agree that any dispute that arises with a volunteer or with this church as a result of participation in the soul-care ministry will be settled by mediation and, if necessary, legally binding arbitration in accordance with the Rules of Procedure of the Institute for Christian Conciliation and any judgment upon an arbitration award may be entered in any court having jurisdiction. We will be happy to provide you with a Web site or documentation that explains the Christian conciliation process and describe its benefits and procedure.

## Agreement

Having read the foregoing information fully and completely, I agree to discuss any questions I may have with the soul-care staff or volunteer to my satisfaction before I begin. My signature below indicates that I understand all the material presented and fully agree to comply.

Name: _____
*(please print)*

Signature: _____

Date: _____

Signature of Parent or Guardian: _____
*(if participant is under 18)*

Witness: _____

*Permission is granted by the publisher to reproduce this page for your ministry.*

SECTION 4

# RESOURCES FOR
## *a Full-Orbed*
# SOUL-CARE MINISTRY
## IN YOUR CHURCH

What is the viability and validity of our current
institutional arrangements? What are the implications
for the church of Christ when its designated or presumed
experts in the cure of souls are state-licenses, fee-
for-service, mental health professional without any
organic linkage to ecclesiastical oversight? What are the
implications for the Church of Christ or its current lack
of many crucial institutional structures that are necessary
for caring for souls?.

—DAVID POWLISON, "Cure of Souls," *The Journal of Biblical Counseling*

# OUTSOURCING—
# DEEP
# *Spiritual*
# RISKS

Pastors have gradually noticed that those who receive care from secular mental health workers end up living in two different worlds—one secular or psychological, the other God-centered—and the psychological emphasis usually dominates. It is axiomatic that counselees, given enough time, adopt the worldview of their counselor. The result is that the gospel is relegated to a smaller and smaller sector of a person's world.

—EDWARD WELCH, *The Journal of Biblical Counseling*

*"Beware of false prophets who come to you in sheep's clothing but inwardly are ravaging wolves. You'll recognize them by their fruit. Are grapes gathered from thornbushes or figs from thistles? In the same way, every good tree produces good fruit, but a bad tree produces bad fruit."*
—MATTHEW 7:15-17

# TAPPING INTO THE EXPERTS

Serendipity's Picking Up the Pieces healing and recovery series provides powerful, practical tools that are part of an effective soul-care ministry strategy. The strategy in this handbook is straightforward and biblical, but it's not always easy. Humans are complex, and complex problems are not solved with simplistic solutions. Some in the church say that if we correct the sin issue, the resulting emotional illness will correct itself. Is it this simple? In many cases it is not; even in those cases where personal sin is the central issue, multiple related issues such as difficult life situations, wounded hearts, embedded lies, enemy strongholds, and a history of harmful coping strategies demand attention. If we try to address deep and complex problems of the heart with simplistic answers, then we fall into the same trap as many secular therapists: we try to stop arterial bleeding with Band-Aids.

Radio, television, and self-help books are replete with "experts" touting "easy steps" to answer deep and complex problems of the heart. Answers that require a few outward changes and no internal transformation certainly appeal to our human nature. Unfortunately, these messages have also become the mantra of some popular Christian authors and counselors. The "name it and claim it" self-esteem gospel in many Christian self-help books directs us to a cheap self-aggrandizing form of Christianity. This distorted brand of Christianity encourages us to look on the bright side of life without telling us that the only bright side available is the one we find through deep connection with Jesus Christ and others who follow Him.

God strongly criticized the prophets and priests of the Old Testament for applying superficial bandages to deep emotional and spiritual wounds: "They have treated My people's brokenness superficially, claiming: Peace, peace, when there is no peace" (Jer. 6:14). We cannot gloss over people's pain and misery persuading them they will easily be cured. Healing is often a difficult process that requires trust, authenticity, and grace within the context of relationship—with God and with His people.

> Beware of preaching the gospel of temperament instead of the gospel of God. . . . Thank God He does alter the heart, and when His new life is in our hearts, we can work it out through our heads and express it in our lives.
>
> —OSWALD CHAMBERS, *Biblical Psychology*

Pastors and ministers can become overwhelmed as church members seek them out in times of need. Because of their inability to handle the volume and complexity of the issues their people face and due to lack of training or perceived incompetence, many pastors and churches have opted to outsource the practice of soul care to professionals in the mental health field. Outsourcing or referral to secular and Christian counselors has become the rule rather than the exception.

## We Don't See the Dangers

How can the church deal with those who are hurting, depressed, and or dealing with severe emotional issues without a wholesale acceptance of philosophies antithetical to the Christian faith? Pastors have been too quick to depend on professionals grounded in philosophies incompatible with Christian faith, exposing people to secular humanism. The church must address the question of professional counseling and its social structure for delivering soul care. We must also guide and examine the content and theory of Christian counseling. A counselor's view of God and human nature, as well as his or her approach, will align the counseling endeavor toward truth or error.

I am a licensed clinical psychologist, and I want to make clear that I'm not bashing psychology. There is, however, concern for psychology as it relates to our discussion about soul care. Psychology has developed skills and methodologies for relating to people in the practice of counseling that conservative theologians applaud. However, there are critical implications when psychology has been impacted by philosophies and culture inconsistent with biblical truth. The mental health industry has an organizational, philosophical, and financial structure that is often inconsistent with the purposes of the local church. Independent professional counselors have a defective professional and financial structure if they operate under a secular managed-care paradigm.

## Unveiling Contemporary Psychology

Contemporary psychology is a system of theories and techniques for the purpose of diagnosing and treating a myriad of emotional, relational, and mental problems within the context of federal and state jurisprudence. Its practitioners are trained in these methodologies; this is their principle area of expertise.

Psychology does offer valuable empirical and anecdotal information about how people think and behave when they experience developmental, medical, relational, and genetic anomalies. However, a psychology based on theoretical constructs that deny or ignore God is inconsistent with truth and a legitimate Christian faith. We should demand that our counsel be biblical. A biblical or Christian psychology would take into account teachings regarding God, Satan's sabotage of mankind, man's fall, and the entry of sin and rebellion in our world as causes of human suffering. Such a Christian worldview only serves to increase our awareness of sin or woundedness and lead us to see our desperate, ongoing need for a Savior and Redeemer.

Recent secular movements have included humanism, existentialism, and the importance of individual freedom. This worldview shift has put more emphasis on self and less on God. The logical outcome of this mind-set is apparent today: many believe man's reason and experience define reality so *moral relativism* dominates our culture today. We also see the move toward *individualism*. Individualism is in direct contrast to Christian community. While the Bible does promote individual choice and responsibility, God designed us to live in relationship with other believers. Community is core to biblical faith and personal well-being. We are called to be "one body" throughout the epistles; we are our "brother's keeper" and instructed to treat others as more important than ourselves. In secular psychology the importance of relationships and community has been trumped by the "right" of self-expression and individual freedom, regardless of the impact one's acts or attitudes may have on other people.

> *In secular psychology the importance of relationships and community has been trumped by the "right" of self-expression and individual freedom.*

Because we have lost our moral compass, it is now acceptable to project responsibility for our shortcomings, failures, and sins onto any number of individuals or circumstances—environment, family, poverty, the government, coworkers, and the list goes on. We can do what we want and avoid responsibility for the negative results. Humanistic psychological theory does much to avoid personal responsibility for wrongdoing or wrong thinking. It has become a system with multiple subsystems. Secular assumptions are based on man's attempt to explain his pain without understanding the unseen spiritual dimension. It does not take into account the damaged relationships we have with God and other people because of this fallen world and sin. While highlighting individualism, humanistic therapy avoids assigning a person responsibility for his thought processes and behavior. These systems of psychology are some of the vain and empty philosophies of which we're warned in Colossians 2:8, and in some instances the church has been taken captive.

> *Be careful that no one takes you captive through philosophy and empty deceit based on human tradition, based on the elemental forces of the world, and not based on Christ.*
>
> —COLOSSIANS 2:8

My stand against contemporary psychology may appear to be harsh. I absolutely do stand against the philosophical underpinnings in the discipline that reinforces the radical relativism that's permeating our culture, including our Christian culture. I also stand against the notion that two fundamentally differing "truths" can come together in agreement about God's presence and power and the nature and plight of mankind. To assume that a psychology based on secular humanism (man is the measure of all things) can in any way be consistent with biblical truth is conceptually naïve.

While we must be careful, I also believe there's value to the study of psychology *if* examined critically through the lens of Scripture. Psychology offers protocols and approaches to problem solving that are helpful to the biblical counselor. There have been significant advancements in neuropsychology, learning theory, cognitive functioning, and other related areas. However, we must examine any approach in light of God's revealed truth.

> *The mainstream mental health industry bases its work on symptom reduction and theories that don't acknowledge God.*

The mainstream mental health industry bases its work on symptom reduction and theories that don't acknowledge God or His redemption. While there clearly is a place for professional counseling, my concern is that the church has little or no influence in the soul care of its members who are outsourced to professionals. As a result, the church abdicates its role as the authoritative institution for soul care.

## WE HAVE A LIVING REDEEMER!

Good treatment follows good diagnosis. By God's Spirit through Scripture, we know that we're born into sin, saved by grace through faith, and destined to recover the original glory for which we were created. Jesus Christ is our only hope for newness of life, healing, redemption, and glory—now and then fully realized in eternity. Whatever the cost, we all must be advocates and supporters of truth. God is both the Author and the Sustainer of truth, and His word in Scripture is our ultimate truth source.

We must defend His truth against any philosophy, theory, or system that contradicts His nature, the nature of man, or the larger story of redemption and restoration. While psychology can be helpful, it will never make anyone a totally new creation, give a life of overflowing abundance, set a person free from those things that hold our hearts captive, or lead to a future that's beyond imagination. Only faith in Jesus Christ and the powerful presence of God's Spirit within us gives us access to divinely powerful resources.

The Bible offers a model of soul care that secular practitioners cannot approach in their most expansive fantasies. The Bible focuses on a living Redeemer with total authority over life, death, fear, and bondage. Jesus and His apostles directed the local church to develop a healthy community where suffering and joy can be shared, acceptance is the norm, and truth is the standard. The message of secular counseling is limited and at times misguided, while the competent Christian counselor provides the ultimate good news for transformation and healing.

*I know my living Redeemer, and He will stand on the dust at last.*
—JOB 19:25

# WHAT ABOUT PROFESSIONAL CHRISTIAN COUNSELORS?

Counseling practice and theology must be rightly wedded for the result to strengthen faith and Christian community. The use of secular theories or psychologies to define causation for human suffering is confusing, unwise, and at odds with Scripture. They're woefully inadequate according to our worldview. Yet independent Christian counselors are serving a pastoral role with couples in crisis, people suffering from unrecognized sin, people who are depressed and anxious, and those seeking guidance amid complicated questions. Christian counselors are doing the work of ministry. While they in fact do the work of ministry, they are not examined as thoroughly as a minister who joins a church staff. In fact, many counselors operate without any interactions or connections with the church.

> Like any theological commitment, this comes replete with practical implications. First, Christian counseling is not a distinct entity, but is subsumed under the larger category of pastoral care. It is subject to the same criteria as that of the ordained ministry. Certainly, some are more gifted in personal ministry than others, and some have more experience with the unusual personal problems, but all personal ministry for Christians is ministry of the word of Scripture and the Word—Jesus Christ.
>
> —EDWARD WELCH, *The Journal of Biblical Counseling*

Professional Christian counselors have become a new category of Christian work. In most situations the relationship between the local church and an autonomous, state-accredited, fee-for-service profession remains tenuous. This reality offers the local church an incredible opportunity for institutional innovation in church and parachurch structures. A true parachurch ministry supports and strengthens the local body. An independently functioning, professional Christian, operating *outside* doctrinal and theological oversight, may well weaken the local church by confusing counselees in matters of faith and doctrine. A professional soul-care ministry operating autonomously from the local church is really an anomaly. God's designated soul-care center is the local church.

## MANAGED CARE, MISMANAGED LIVES

Apart from theological and church issues, there are systemic problems. Professional Christian counselors are burdened in ways similar to medical doctors by inherent professional and financial structures. Currently, the term *psychology* (similarly with counseling) is most often used to describe a discipline within the current complex mental health industry. The engine of this industry runs on money regulated by gatekeepers who determine which professional a soul in agony may see. Mental health benefits are part of most people's health insurance, and for Christians this can be a delicate issue. What if you want to see a professional Christian counselor who's not on your insurance company's approved list of clinicians? What if you are in need of counseling for several months, but the gatekeepers will only approve a few sessions? What if the counselors on this list have a worldview that's incompatible with yours?

There are other related concerns. Naturally, insurance companies want to keep their expenditures to a minimum. Medical and mental health professionals are required to get approval for treatments and procedures. Approval usually takes place over the phone with a person who has never seen the patient or counselee. Certain symptoms must be present for the patient or counselee to qualify for more expensive or intensive treatments. Dealing with the human soul is not often as clear-cut as dealing with a diseased body. We should be fully informed about how managed care works so that if the need arises for professional soul care, we can make the best decision for ourselves or our loved ones.

Because of health insurance contracts with managed-care companies (MCOs), a large segment of professional counseling focuses on the external manifestation of an underlying problem—the symptom not the cause. Licensed psychologists and counselors are given criteria they must follow according to their contractual arrangements with MCOs. For the most part these criteria have to do with a reduction in the observable symptoms of a diagnosed problem such as depression or anxiety. Specific criteria are established for each psychological condition. Once the symptoms diminish in the counselee, the counseling task is considered complete, and funds for further counseling may no longer be available from the insurer.

> Today there are more trained mental health clinicians than ever before in our history. Today there are more diagnosed mental health issues than ever before in our history. What's wrong with this picture?

The implication here is significant. The cause of the symptoms may not be addressed, and the method of counseling is controlled to a great degree by what the MCOs are willing to pay. Underlying issues of the heart, which produce the symptoms, are seldom resolved. The counselor has an ethical obligation to the counselee but also a financial relationship with an organization primarily concerned with minimizing its financial outlay. By definition this form of soul care is superficial and is far less likely to lead people toward healing and redemption.

# Rethinking Professional Soul Care

Over decades the church has drifted away from its role in the care and healing of souls. We must reexamine our theological and practical approach to helping the hurting in our churches. With the support and leadership of Christian scholars, theologians, and Christ-centered counselors, we can confront the church's history of passivity in this vital area. Christian counselors have come to grips with the fact that our past success ratios are no better than those of secular counselors. In a way that only God could orchestrate, varied and unconnected healing movements have been arising within many scattered pockets in churches and among Christian counselors. With God's leading and direction, many disconnected movements and events are coming together, and we're poised to begin the process of taking back what we relinquished to the world in the 1950s.

> *It's time to reexamine our theological and practical approach to helping the hurting in our churches.*

It's becoming clear to most churches that a bad theology of soul care has produced a bad result. A good (biblical) theology of soul care clearly demonstrates that a division between spiritual and psychological is artificial. Of course, we won't be equipped to deal with the most severe problems within the church, and yet we cannot outsource our soul care to the spirit of the world without grave consequences. The spirit of the world has permeated secular counseling theories, and our therapeutic culture promotes "self-life." When we try to identify and resolve spiritual issues using humanistic, man-centric ideologies, we're introducing the spirit of the world into the church. We should use wisdom generated in the world, but our ultimate source of wisdom and power must be from the Spirit of God.

> The Lord whose gaze and will the Bible reveals lays claim to the cure of souls. If counseling is indeed about understanding and resolving the human condition, if it deals with the real problems of real people, if it ever mentions the name of Jesus Christ, then it traffics in theology and cure of souls; it ought to express and come under the church's authority and orthodoxy.
>
> —David Powlison, *The Journal of Biblical Counseling*

We can do much in the church to prevent our members from entering a system that does not view the world the same way we do. A pastor and a people with a heart for tending and feeding the sheep can take care of much human pain, suffering, and confusion. We can even have a positive effect on professionals since many depend on referrals. The church can and should be the soul-care center for church members.

By now you're beginning to see clearly the dangers of outsourcing soul care. Your enthusiasm is likely growing as you realize the hope of recapturing this vital area. The solution is primarily one of changing people's mind-sets and changing our structures. We must reclaim the responsibility and authority given us by the God who created us. We must have no fear to proclaim the gospel of Jesus Christ or its role in the redemption of relationships. We need not operate in fear; instead we should move forward with a holy boldness. We have a biblical mandate to be in the business of soul care.

## TOGETHER WE NEED TO LEAD THE WAY

The church should be leading the way into frontiers of the care and healing of the soul. We rightly claim Christ is the cure, and His followers are to provide His care. Yet we've allowed other "experts" to come in and do our work. We've often focused on what to do and what not to do instead of on our true identity in Christ and our ongoing redemptive, relational journey with the Almighty God of the universe who calls us His sons and His beloved. Beyond that, we've sacrificed authentic relationship and redemptive community for comfort. Fellowship and relationship become superficial and comfortable when we refuse to enter one another's pain. We've allowed a void to be created in the lives of our people, and a proliferation of New Age and humanistic philosophies have been all too willing to move into our neighborhoods.

> *We've sacrificed authentic relationships and redemptive community for comfort.*

The care and healing of souls has been the responsibility of the local church from the beginning. The rise of professionalism and secular psychologies in the 19th and 20th centuries effectively reduced the church's involvement in this vital area. Unfortunately, we have quietly allowed the souls of the redeemed to be turned over to those who reject the notion of God as the Bible reveals Him.

We have an uncomplicated model presented in this handbook that places the local church back in its God-appointed role. We can equip the saints to do God's work in the lives of the hurting. Our pastors can oversee the flock and hold professionals accountable when problems are severe or medically related. All we have to do is implement the structures, train the people, and do the work of ministry.

# BALANCING
# PROFESSIONAL
# INTERVENTION
## *in the*
# CHURCH

Some Christians believe there are marvelous things to learn from modern psychology, embracing psychological findings and theories with enthusiasm, while others approach secular psychology with great caution.

—ERIC L. JOHNSON AND STANTON L. JONES, *Psychology and Christianity*

> Now may the God of peace Himself sanctify you completely.
> And may your spirit, soul, and body be kept sound and blameless
> for the coming of our Lord Jesus Christ.
> —1 THESSALONIANS 5:23

# A Place for Professional Intervention in the Church

Legitimate mental illness does exist in the church. Depression, anxiety, bipolar disorder, schizophrenia, and other maladies likely have a physiological basis and/or a relationship with neurological or biochemical interactions. Emotional problems may also be the result of past trauma, false beliefs deeply embedded in our hearts, unresolved or unrepented sin, poor decision-making, spiritual oppression, or a combination of factors. In many cases these issues are seldom treated effectively with counseling alone. Some of these infirmities severely affect cognitive functioning and prevent the appropriation of truth.

## Treating the Whole Person

We cannot compartmentalize human beings. It's conceptually naïve to treat any sphere of our being in isolation from the other parts. Even current medical science provides empirical evidence that spotlights the error of compartmentalization. We know that continued physical distress will result in emotional problems. Emotional problems do in fact affect our physical well-being.

Historical biblical orthodoxy attests that the Trinity functions with an "essential unity," even though not all would necessarily use this specific term. The absolute oneness of God is summed up in opening phrase of the Jewish Shema in Deuteronomy 6:4. An accurate biblical anthropology clearly demonstrates that there is also an "essential unity" among three "parts" of human beings. We cannot separate body, soul, and spirit, even though each has a distinct function according to God's plan and design. Deuteronomy 6:4 refers to man as containing heart, soul, and strength. Jesus affirmed the essence of all the commandments is summed up in loving God with everything we have—"with all your heart, with all your soul, and with all your mind, and with all your strength" (Mark 12:30)—and loving our neighbors as ourselves.

> Listen, Israel: The LORD our God, the LORD is one. Love the LORD your God with all your heart, with all your soul, and with all your strength.
>
> —Deuteronomy 6:4-5

Human beings are not one-dimensional. The Bible teaches that we have a spirit, a soul (mind, emotion, and will), and a body. None of these dimensions operates in isolation, and all are affected by sin. We know that severe emotional stress can result in medical problems. Physical stress, lack of rest, and poor nutrition will influence us emotionally. Our spiritual condition affects all areas of life, as does the spiritual warfare blazing within us. Any counsel focusing in an overly simplistic fashion on one of these dimensions of man without consideration of the whole person ultimately could cause more harm than good.

## Responsible Use of Medications

While some pastors and Christian counselors oppose the use of medication in any situation, others do not. Medication should be prescribed in a responsible manner when indicated due to a true medical or psychological condition. For those enduring severe emotional and cognitive distortions, it is merciful to use medication properly. Would we withhold antibiotics from a person with a severe staph infection or drugs from a person with cancer? Often counseling can be augmented with the use of medication when treating medically linked emotional and spiritual issues. We desperately need more study and dialogue in this area. The responsible use of medication is no easy task unless we're willing to compartmentalize humankind and ignore that all dimensions of a life are interrelated.

## Wounds No One Can See

Women who have postpartum depression feel a triple whammy of the stigma reserved for people with mental illnesses. Not only are they brought down by what many expect to be the happiest event in a woman's life—the birth of a child—but also total honesty about their emotional state could invite scorn or even a visit from social services. Crippling sleep deprivation and the isolation of being home with a newborn compound the problem.

When Katherine Stone, 38, of Atlanta had images of her baby son drowning in the bathtub or being smothered on his burp cloth, she feared for her sanity. But she kept it from her husband as long as she could. Six years later the mother of two still feels judged for taking antidepressants for postpartum depression, and she believes there is a common misperception that depressed mothers are self-centered and weak.

"We're suffering from an illness that cannot be seen," Stone says. "We don't have a fever, swelling, vomiting, or diarrhea. No open wounds that will not heal—at least not the kind you can see with the naked eye. So, many wonder if we're really sick at all."

A growing body of evidence finds that medications and other treatments can mitigate or even reverse postpartum mood disorders. The trick is finding a health professional who specializes in treating it and who won't brush you off with a pep talk. Yes, the depression may go away on its own, but waiting can put the whole family in jeopardy.

Drugs should not be used to mask the symptoms of deeper emotional or spiritual issues. Psychopharmacology cannot correct the heart or resolve life issues. However, to state generically that the use of medication is bad or that the medical community should use drugs without accountability or accurate diagnosis are different sides of the same coin. Radical support of either position is a dangerous form of reductionism. Christian counselors, psychologists, and even pastors should have a working knowledge of neurophysiology—how emotional and spiritual issues affect thinking and mood. The physician should consider the consequences of using a drug to deal with complex issues, or symptoms having spiritual and emotional dimensions, without assistance or accountability. We must function as healing teams, with diverse members adding unique gifts and expertise.

## Just Medicate it Away

*I have a friend whose son was adopted from an orphanage overseas. His son has been rightly diagnosed with severe ADHD. Because of the complexity of this boy's issues, the physician referred him to a psychiatrist. With his greater knowledge of the biochemical issues, the psychiatrist found the best combination of medications to settle the boy down enough to focus, which helped him to perform better in school and at home. The parents were thankful for the help of the medication but remained concerned about their son's deep-seated issues related to self-centeredness, manipulation, and aggressiveness—probably connected to living nearly four years in an orphanage. Even when asked repeatedly, the psychiatrist met only once with the boy for talk therapy and then dismissed the concerns, saying, "Let's just keep him on the medications, and I think he'll do OK." In the end the parents concluded that the psychiatrist really had no idea how to address these "ideas and thoughts of the heart" (Heb. 4:12).*

## Church as the Primary Soul-Care Center

The church has a moral obligation for the care and healing of souls. While we may not be equipped to deal with complicated medical or psychological problems, the vast majority of Christ followers' problems can and should be dealt with in the church. The following illustration demonstrates in a general way how the church can and should act as the primary soul-care provider for its members.

**CHURCH**
SOUL CARE AND CURE
*Marriage, Parenting, Conflict,*
*Grief, Loss, Sexual Sin,*
*Betrayal, Confusion,*
*Suffering.*
*Etc.*

**SPECIALIZATION REFERRAL**
MEDICAL/
PSYCHOLOGICAL
ILLNESS
· *Schizophrenia*
· *Bipolar*
· *Dementia*
· *Etc.*

**URGENCY REFERRAL**
MEDICAL/
PSYCHOLOGICAL
ILLNESS
· *Suicide Threats*
· *Severe Depression*
· *Life-Threatening*
*Addictions*
· *Etc.*

Even when people are referred, the church has the responsibility to ensure that the professionals responsible for their care operate from a fully Christ-centered, biblical framework; remain theologically and doctrinally consistent with the referring church; and communicate with those providing follow-up soul care in the church.

> *The church has a legal right and moral obligation for the healing*
> *and care of souls.*

## NOTES

1. "Why You Can't Wait to Treat Postpartum Depression," *www.health.com/health/ condition-article/0,,20188712,00.html*, accessed October 21, 2008.

# IN-HOUSE
# COUNSELING—
## *Liability*
# RISKS

The Bible does locate care and cure in the body of Christ. But the church in reality does not have institutional structures in place to deliver the goods. Functional autonomy and potential for confusion and error are not only problems of mental health professionalism. Within the church herself, cure of souls operates in almost identical autonomy, with almost identical potential for theological and practical trouble.

—David Powlison

*Which of you, wanting to build a tower, doesn't first sit down and calculate the cost to see if he has enough to complete it? Otherwise, after he has laid the foundation and cannot finish it, all the onlookers will begin to make fun of him.*

—Luke 14:28-29

Earlier we focused on the dangers associated with outsourcing soul care to the professionals. Through the rise of humanism and relativism, we have unwittingly allowed the souls of the redeemed to be turned over to those who reject the notion of God as the Bible reveals Him. The key lessons we emphasized were:

1. Ecclesiastical oversight of soul care is required.
2. Heart transformation occurs in a ministry model, not a secular managed-care structure.
3. Soul care must be Christ centered, Spirit directed, and biblically grounded.

The church has a legal right, a moral obligation, and a spiritual mandate for the care and healing of souls. While we may not be equipped to deal with severe medical or psychological problems, the vast majority of problems Christ followers face can and should be addressed in the church. Even when members are referred, the church should do all it can to ensure that the professionals responsible for their care operate from a Christian worldview and if possible maintain communication with the counselor so ministry care and professional care are consistent. If the church has the appropriate structure for soul care and stays within it, risk and liability are minimized. The risks highlighted in this chapter are important to consider, but they should not keep us from bringing soul care back into the domain of the church.

> *Now everything is from God, who reconciled us to Himself through Christ and gave us the ministry of reconciliation: that is, in Christ, God was reconciling the world to Himself, not counting their trespasses against them, and He has committed the message of reconciliation to us.*
> —2 CORINTHIANS 5:18-19

## OPENING A DIFFERENT CAN OF WORMS

More and more churches are becoming aware of the significant risks involved in outsourcing the soul care of our hurting members. In many conservative and evangelical circles, concern is growing about ecclesiastical oversight. To address this concern, many churches able to allocate the funds think bringing licensed counselors into the church as staff members remedies their issues. While this approach may give the church some sense of security about the nature of the counseling members receive, it opens up a legal can of worms of which most are unaware.

Let me give you an example. In the U.S., a church's "normal and customary function" (this is a legal phrase) is to minister to people within the context of doctrines, theological beliefs, matters of faith, and relationships with God and other church members. Other areas within normal and customary function relate to the mission and vision of the denomination and the local church. Legally the state does not have an entry point into a church's practice of religion—its normal and customary function—unless a church does something negligent like avoiding mandatory reporting laws, overstepping its boundaries as a religious institution, or sexual harassment/abuse. However, persons licensed by the state have a primary fiduciary responsibility to the state, the statutes in the state relating to their profession, and the particular associations to which they belong. So if a licensed professional is employed by a church, the state can pierce the corporate veil of the church in the case of a malpractice or negligence claim against the professional. This weakens or eliminates the protection of church autonomy that's guaranteed under the constitution and federal, state, and local laws.

> *Any entity employing professionals licensed by the state must operate according to the ethical and legal guidelines as prescribed by that state. The licensee's primary fiduciary responsibility will be to the ethical and legal codes determined by licensing bodies in the state. These ethical and legal codes may at times be in conflict with the church's stated beliefs and orthodoxy.*

A church soul-care ministry (a true "in-house" ministry effort driven by pastoral staff and laity) that operates solely within the mission and guidelines of the church has no legal or ethical responsibility to state licensing boards for professionals. While licensed professionals may perform soul-care duties within the church, precautions must be taken to inform, both verbally and in writing, all those receiving soul care that the "service or ministry" they're receiving is *not* professional. The forms and other tools in this book can help you with this communication.

To separate legally the ministerial functions from the professional, the professional counseling group should be a separate legal entity. If a church hires a licensed professional and bills for professional services performed, it may be operating outside its corporate structures or constitution and bylaws. In addition, if the church is charging for the services of an "employee," the church's not-for-profit status could be in jeopardy. When a separate legal entity is formed and employs professional counselors, enough degrees of separation are created to protect the church in case one of the counselors acts unprofessionally or is a plaintiff in a lawsuit.

## LACK OF ACCOUNTABILITY

I've consulted with many churches over the years, helping them develop soul-care ministries in the form of *topic-specific group ministries, intensive discipleship initiates*, and *biblical or pastoral counseling*. The most important dynamic in providing soul care in any form is to define clearly the relationship between the participant and the one leading or providing the care.

I've also worked with other churches that had a heart for the care and healing of the souls of its members. These churches focused on extensive *topic-specific group ministries*, *one-on-one counseling*, and varied *strategic discipleship venues*. Unfortunately, some of these churches paid too little attention to accountability or liability, putting both the church and its members at risk. Many of the group leaders were operating independently, making referrals and giving advice that was clearly inconsistent with the church's doctrine or theological positions. Many of the resource materials were also inconsistent from a doctrinal or theological position. There was often no group leader selection process, and most of the people leading groups had not been through any formal training. While intentions were outstanding, the structure and procedures provided little, if any, accountability and guidance. All of these concerns create legal risk for a church and potential harm to its members.

## INCREASING LITIGATION AGAINST CHURCHES

According to attorney Stephen Chawaga in *Your Church* magazine, "There was a time when the most significant lawsuit a church had to fear was from someone who slipped on the sidewalk in front of the entrance. Even then, the church might have escaped liability because of a statutory or judicial grant of immunity. Those days are now gone, as it seems that new causes for action against religious institutions are being invented daily.[1]

Society's preoccupation with individualism has also contributed to the increase in litigation in Western countries, as has our diminished respect for authority and our embracing of relative morality. These changing attitudes have resulted in a general antagonism toward the concepts of responsibility, accountability, and discipline found in the church.

## CURRENT RISKS IN CHURCH-RELATED COUNSELING[2]

The following list compiles the top 10 risk factors churches face today related to in-house counseling or soul care. Practical and easy-to-implement solutions will be provided in later chapters of the handbook.

1. INADEQUATE REGISTRATION/INFORMED-CONSENT FORMS—Unclearly defined expectations and boundaries between counselor and counselee decrease effectiveness and expose the church to litigation.
2. FAILURE TO DEFINE RELATIONSHIPS CLEARLY—Relationships between counselor, church leaders, and counselee are not often defined in informed-consent forms—including liability, confidentiality, and church discipline issues.

3. UNAUTHORIZED COUNSELING WITHOUT A LICENSE—Church staff or lay counselors might deal with situations for which they have insufficient training, use the unauthorized practice of psychology or counseling without a license, or do not make the appropriate referrals. Without clearly defined scope and standards, a referral list, and ongoing supervision, we set ourselves up for problems. This issue was challenged in *Grace Community vs. McNally*. Although Grace Community was eventually exonerated, the suit lasted 10 years, and the expense to the church was great.

4. INADEQUATE TRAINING/SUPERVISION OF LAY VOLUNTEERS—The church is optimally protected when ordained ministers counsel and give advice within church doctrine and matters of faith (normal and customary functions of a church). The next highest level of protection is with paid staff. The lowest level of protection is with lay counselors. Lay counselors, with appropriate training and supervision, should be transitioned into mentoring/discipleship roles.

5. COUNSELING NOT DISTINCTIVELY DIFFERENT FROM SECULAR COUNSELING—At the AACC World Conference in 2001, Dr. Miriam Parent said, "Christian counseling must involve more than a prayer at the beginning and end of the session." The church can be held to the highest secular standard of the American Psychological Association if there's no clear distinction in Christian counseling. Biblically based, Christ-centered counseling is distinctive, and this must be made clear in the first meeting with a person and documented via an informed consent form.

6. INADEQUATE MALPRACTICE OR LIABILITY INSURANCE—Insurance is required for individuals who have major counseling responsibilities (staff and members).

7. INADEQUATE GUIDELINES REGARDING REPORTING ABUSE—Even with confidentiality protection, it's necessary to follow state and federal guidelines for reporting abuse.

8. INSUFFICIENT DOCUMENTATION—Thorough documentation of counseling appointments, phone conversations, and all counselee contact is required to fend off potential lawsuits.

9. LACK OF FORMAL SUPERVISION AND/OR CONSULTING RELATIONSHIPS WITH A LICENSED PROFESSIONAL

10. THE ABSENCE OF PRACTICAL ACCOUNTABILITY MEASURES—Examples include windows on doors and regular staff meetings to share issues that arise in counseling situations.

> *The most important dynamic in providing soul care in any form is to define clearly the relationship between the participant and the one leading or providing the care.*

Losing a lawsuit can result in devastating damages. These damages in time, money, and disruption of the church's primary mission may take years to overcome. Even when a church wins in court, it usually pays an enormous price in terms of legal fees, lost time and energy, distraction from ministry, and congregational dissension over the underlying causes of the conflict. Awards against churches receive unwanted media coverage and do much to harm the cause of Christ. A pastor and officers of the church still can be found to be personally liable for damages awarded in lawsuits related to counseling, confidentiality, sexual misconduct, or church discipline even if the church is incorporated. If insurance does not cover the entire award, a prevailing plaintiff can recover his damages from a single church leader, who may then be compelled to sue his fellow officers to force them to share that cost. Before a church enters into helping those with damaged souls, it needs to be wise in laying the foundation and preparation.

I became aware of a large evangelical church that hired licensed professionals to provide counseling. These licensed professional counselors owed primary fiduciary responsibility to the state and the board who licensed them. The church, a not-for-profit corporation, employed these licensed professionals and billed a fee for their professional services. Further, this church did little to examine these counselors theologically or personally. No one really knew what transpired behind closed doors when members of the congregation were counseled. The liability issues in this situation were tremendous.

The best-case scenario would have been for the church to develop a true soul-care ministry. The church would have conducted ministry—not professional counseling regulated by a ton of laws (e.g. confidentiality versus privilege). This would have eliminated entry points for the state or federal government.

I was later contacted by the leaders of the church because of their concerns related to the church's liability. We suspended fees, began teaching the pastors how to provide soul care within the scope of their calling and the church's mission, and created a separate legal entity for the counselors. Training for pastoral staff and laity in the ministry of soul care is progressing.

The professional counselors who remained went through 14 months of intensive training and supervision to ensure they are now providing sound Christ-centered care. This organization of professional counselors supports multiple local churches through training and emergency response; it has become a true parachurch ministry. Liability issues have been greatly reduced, and there is a seamless relationship between the professional soul-care ministry and multiple local churches.

## Risk of Losing Tax-Exempt Status

Most churches in the U.S. are 501C3s (not-for-profit corporations) that receive donations (tithes and gifts) from their members to fund ministries. Ministry is within the scope of what a church is all about. Churches hire ministers, those called and gifted to minister. They operate from a biblical and theological perspective. They provide the love, support, and encouragement of our Lord Jesus Christ and the gospel. Fee-for-service, professional counselors conducting business as employees of the church "corporation" expose their churches to unnecessary risk and liability. Beyond exposing the church to liability and malpractice claims against professionals, this fee-based approach could place the church's status as a not-for-profit corporation in jeopardy.[3]

> *Fee-for-service, professional counselors working within the church could place the church's status as a not-for-profit corporation in jeopardy.*

In another large church the pastoral staff had been overwhelmed with counseling requests, many too complicated for their level of experience and training. This church was to be applauded for being one of the early churches in the 1980s to demonstrate love and take action to care for its members. They established a Christian counseling center within the church that remained active over several years. The church hired a clinical psychologist and several other licensed counselors to begin a full counseling ministry in the church.

Church leaders were unaware of the liability or risk associated with such a venture. The church board, concerned about legal liability, contacted me knowing that I was experienced in this area. This church operated a fee-for-service professional counseling entity within the context of the church ministry, and they were fortunate to avoid lawsuits and loss of tax-exempt status.

In addition to the legal risks involved, this model opened the church to governmental controls they did not want. This professional in-house model operated inconsistently with both the mission and the vision of the church. The counseling entity, while legally part of the church, was not integrated within a churchwide strategy, nor was it operated with appropriate ministerial oversight. Fees were immediately suspended to reduce risk, and then the church moved to adopt the model espoused in this book.

In the two church stories in this chapter, the ministry involving lay members in soul care, discipleship and group leadership could not begin until professionals were moved into another legal entity. It is not wise to blur the lines between ministry and professional counseling. However, with appropriate ecclesiastical oversight, the professional entity and the church soul-care ministry should work in tandem for full congregational and community impact. Neither will be as effective if they function in isolation.

> *The church soul-care ministry and the professional ministry must work in tandem for full congregational and community impact.*

## Why a Not-for-Profit Ministry?

The not-for-profit status is intentional. This model can succeed financially while still serving those who don't have the finances for counseling when a crisis occurs. It's much easier to establish a "for profit" legal entity for professional counselors, even Christian counselors. Whenever you have a profit motive (based on the structure of the business entity) and a ministry motive, the profit motive will take precedence. A not-for-profit entity can be more complex due to increased accountability, but it provides the necessary structure to ensure the ministry motive triumphs. It also provides a benefit for churches and individuals who wish to donate money to support the ministry.

Many Christian counselors and centers provide a sliding-scale fee in an effort to assist those with limited resources. While the desire to assist those in need should be applauded, at HeartLife Professional Soul-Care, we found this method cumbersome and without necessary accountability. We established a benevolence fund to assist counselees without financial resources. We require them to fill out an application, which provides us with the level of need and the patterns that may indicate lifestyle issues related to stewardship. We often make our benevolence assistance dependent on the applicant's also seeking financial counseling. We have a list of financial counselors who perform this service at no charge. Through this and other criteria, we try to ensure that all applicants are treated fairly in the distribution of funds and that they deal with all the issues that may be contributing to their problems.

Other practical examples can be obtained on our Web site—*www.heartlifesoulcare.org*.

## Let's Be Informed and Intentional

Jim Wallace, president and CEO of GuideOne Insurance, said in an interview on Rev.org: "Even though the concept of risk management may seem somewhat out of place in a religious setting . . . risk management is really about good stewardship and safeguarding the people and property that God has entrusted to the church. If risk management is supported by church leaders and programs are properly implemented, safety and security measures can be woven seamlessly into the culture and ministries of the church. Unfortunately, we now live in a world where anything is possible, so the need for risk management has never been greater."

> *Risk management is really about good stewardship and safeguarding the people and property God has entrusted to the church.*

Clearly risk management for soul-care ministry must be evaluated as part of any church's overall risk management evaluation and corrective action set. The legal realities identified in this chapter are dramatically minimized by implementing the model I'm unwrapping in this book.

The legal information is as close as the keyboard on your computer. God paints the vision and mission for us in Scripture. The process and steps are in this book. The main ingredient you'll need to add is enthusiastic execution.

> It is not good enough for things to be planned—they still have to be done; for the intention to become a reality, energy has to be launched into operation.

NOTES

1. Stephen Chawaga, "The Ten Deadly Lawsuits," *Your Church*, May/June 2001, vol. 47, no. 3, 55, *www.christianitytoday.com/yc/2001/003/8.55.html*.

2. Compiled from AACC World Conference, *Christianity Today*, Church Law and Tax Report, August 2001; private attorneys currently involved in church litigation; and directors of Southern Baptist church counseling ministries.

3. For more information about the consequences of losing tax exemptions, see *www.christianitytoday.com/cbg/churchlawtax/articles/ask_080918.html*, accessed October 21, 2008.

# OUR
*Soul-Care*
# HERITAGE

Let this mind be in you which was also in Christ Jesus
(Philippians 2:5). There is only one kind of holiness, and
that is the holiness of the Lord Jesus. There is only one
kind of human nature, and that is the human nature of us
all, and Jesus Christ by means of His identification with
our human nature can give us the disposition that He
had. We have to see to it that we habitually work out that
disposition through our eyes and ears and tongues, through
all the organs of our bodies and in every detail of our lives.

—OSWALD CHAMBERS, *Biblical Psychology*

*They devoted themselves to the apostles' teaching, to fellowship,
to the breaking of bread, and to prayers. Then fear came over
everyone, and many wonders and signs were being performed
through the apostles. Now all the believers were together and
had everything in common.*

—ACTS 2:42-44

# Soul Care in the Early Church

Before our discussion of the soul-care revolution, let's build context by taking a look backward at our heritage. Throughout history Christians have looked to God, the Bible, and the church in times of suffering. As God's people, we need His presence, His assurance, and His guidance when we're hurting. Reading Scripture was an essential element when followers of Christ gathered in the early church. Scripture study, community, sacraments, and prayer were prominent in guiding the early Christians to become virtuous. Early Christians considered the Bible and the power of God to be both diagnostic and curative.

Using a metaphor common in his day, Gregory of Nazianzus (A.D. 330-389) saw the pastor as a "physician of souls" who has to treat a sickness found within "the hidden man of the heart," a task more difficult than that of the medical physician because it deals with "the diagnosis and cure of our habits, passions, lives, wills, and whatever else is within us."[1]

> When the Pharisees saw this, they asked His disciples, "Why does your Teacher eat with the tax collectors and sinners?" But when He heard this, He said, "Those who are well don't need a doctor, but the sick do. Go and learn what this means: I desire mercy and not sacrifice. For I didn't come to call the righteous, but sinners."
> —MATTHEW 9:11-13

In his book *Classical Pastoral Care*, Thomas Oden states that pastors in the early church engaged in soul care. He also used a medical metaphor to make his point. The physician metaphor is not complete without the complementary metaphor of guidance. For even one who is well needs a guide through hazardous territory. The soul needs not only a physician for sickness but also a guide through dangerous terrain. In the background of this metaphor is the hazard of the high mountain, the danger of the dark forest, the confusion of the trackless desert, the clamor of the distant city where one does not know the language. To be there without a guide is folly. These are the situations to which the soul's journey is analogous.[2]

> Be on guard for yourselves and for all the flock, among whom the Holy Spirit has appointed you as overseers, to shepherd the church of God, which He purchased with His own blood. I know that after my departure savage wolves will come in among you, not sparing the flock. And men from among yourselves will rise up with deviant doctrines to lure the disciples into following them. Therefore be on the alert, remembering that night and day for three years I did not stop warning each one of you with tears.
> —ACTS 20:28-31

Based on Jesus' passion for the lost and hurting, the cure and care of weary and troubled souls involved communicating God's truth and compassion within the context of relationship. Pastors and church leaders viewed themselves as caretakers of the soul. They were there for their flocks as they encountered the difficulties of life.

According to Ephesians 4:11-16, the church was given special individuals who were gifted to provide spiritual wisdom during times of discouragement, loss, confusion, and heartache. These people were the shepherds and equippers who genuinely cared for the souls of the suffering and ministered to them out of their personal experience of God and an intimate understanding of the Word of God. The modern church has all but abandoned an important biblical goal of getting all the saints involved and equipped in doing works of service.

## The Importance of Christian Community

To be what He intends for us to be, we need fellowship. We are to worship, pray, witness, and share the deepest hurts we experience with one another. Passages such as Romans 12; Ephesians 4; and 1 Corinthians 12–14 show us that our spiritual progress depends on our ability to minister to others. Paul says that we are members of a body; the body moves, lives, and grows together. This illustrates God's pattern for our lives. We belong to a living, praying, worshiping, ministering community of God's people.

In the community of God's people, we must refuse to yield to the darkness in our own soul that engenders disruption and creates strife in our community. We are to be truthful to one another, not merely *speaking truth* to one another but *living openly and honestly* with one another. In Ephesians 4:15 Paul is essentially saying, "Do not live a lie." We are not to use our success or background for advantage. In Paul's day the church was composed of Jews, Gentiles, slaves, and free men and women. It is equally diversified today. Our differences are meant to serve the community, not disrupt it. This diversity of people is meant to build up the members of the church body and to serve the cause of kingdom-building. Any assumption of superiority, right to leadership based on position, or socioeconomic status is destructive to the cause of Christ. Our Lord loved and gave Himself for the church. He was rich in glory, yet He became poor and died a horrible death to secure once and for all the fellowship of God with His people.

We are a community of faith—not in ourselves but in Christ. Christian faith takes its character and quality of fellowship from the object of our faith, Jesus. Our strength does not come from our position or natural abilities but from the power of the risen Christ who holds the power of life and death. Many of us in the community of Christ followers may have weak faith, but we must remember that we have a strong Savior.

# Christian Mysticism

"Although the essence of mysticism is the sense of contact with the transcendent, mysticism in the history of Christianity should *not* be understood merely in terms of special ecstatic experiences but as part of a religious process lived out within the Christian community. From this perspective mysticism played a vital part in the early church."[3]

The letters of Paul and John's Gospel give perhaps the fullest expressions of Christian mysticism in Scriptures. The overarching mystical longing was for union with Christ. Philippians 3:10-11 may well sum up the supreme desire of Paul's heart: "My goal is to know Him and the power of His resurrection and the fellowship of His sufferings, being conformed to His death, assuming that I will somehow reach the resurrection and the fellowship of His sufferings, being conformed to His death." Paul implies personal union, special intimacy, and mutuality experienced within the Trinity.

In John 17:22-24 Jesus prayed about His followers, "I have given them the glory You have given Me. May they be one as We are one. I am in them and You are in Me. May they be made completely one, so the world may know You have sent Me and have loved them as You have loved Me. Father, I desire those You have given Me to be with Me where I am. Then they will see My glory, which You have given Me because You love Me before the world's foundation." The Christ with whom we're united, perfected in unity, is not the man Jesus but the risen, exalted, and glorified I AM.

The essential truths to be gained from Christian mysticism throughout the ages are that we need to experience God personally for transformation to occur, that our inner life drives our outer life, and that soul development is both individual and lived out within a redemptive community.

# Soul Care Through the Centuries

Looking back into the second century, we see the church and Christian leaders abandoning the culture of their day and fervently pursuing God. Through intensive study of the Holy Scriptures, vibrant, redemptive fellowship, and intimate connection to God through prayer and the sacraments, these believers sought to transform their souls and the culture around them. Late in the third century a powerful monastic movement was taking place. This movement had a great impact since Scripture was the primary text used to advance the development of the soul. A good portion of the monk's daily life was engaged with reading and meditating prayerfully on Scripture. "Every monastic order had a 'Rule,' its own guidebook for monastic life, but it was considered subordinate to the Scriptures, and the Rule itself typically required much daily exposure to Scripture through reading, preaching, and hearing, praying and singing.[4]

It's also important to see the value and influence of the monastic structure on soul care and development. Younger members submitted to older members to learn and be transformed by their faith. Perhaps because many of the great Christian authors were members or affiliated with monastic communities, the Bible became the governing text during this period.

While we understand that monastic life is not necessary for us to experience soul transformation, there are some principles of relationship and community on which the modern church doesn't focus enough. The monks lived life in an environment that required each to be concerned about the well-being of the others. They were taught virtues that were lived out communally in an environment that honored God. They were taught to love one another, honor seniors, minister to one another, express charity, and teach the Old and New Testaments accurately. We certainly could benefit from taking a look back to this period in church history.

Perhaps the greatest contribution to soul care occurred during the Reformation. The great reformers focused on the authoritative role of Scripture and recognition of the Bible's impact on the soul. Over the centuries the writings of the church leaders and the church itself became as authoritative as Scripture (this statement is certainly an oversimplification, but a "dual" authority existed).

> All who call on God in true faith, earnestly from the heart, will certainly be heard, and will receive what they have asked and desired.
>
> —MARTIN LUTHER

Prior to the Reformation, most common folk did not read the Bible; their illiteracy and the fact that it had not been translated from Latin were two of the primary reasons. The reformers strongly advocated access to the Bible and interpretation with the Spirit's guidance for common people. The Bible, not merely religious traditions, speaks into the daily lives of people. The focus on the "priesthood of all believers" became a rallying cry along with "sola scriptura"—the Bible alone can be used as our ultimate truth source for Christian doctrine and practice, experiences, revelation, and other extrabiblical information. Needless to say, this period impacted Christianity and the Western world enormously. The Church is still contending over the authority of Scripture, and this issue is central to how we address the care and healing of the soul in the modern church.

## ENTER THE MODERN ERA

As we move forward in history between the 17th and 18th centuries, we see the onset of science and modernism. While some of the originators of modernism and the scientific method considered themselves Christians, their way of thinking challenged Christian intellectual domination in the Western world. Human reason and logic, not faith in an unseen God, became more and more dominant. Empiricism, behaviorism, technological advances, and rationalism began to challenge the authority of biblical revelation. This secular movement soon included humanism, existentialism, and the importance of creative freedom. This worldview shift put more emphasis on self and less on God.

## THE SCIENTIFIC METHOD TRIUMPHS

Biblical soul care, as practiced by our church fathers, changed radically as we entered the 20th century. Prior to the advent of modernism, clergy viewed the care and healing of souls as a crucial component of their pastoral duties. The fall of man and the presence of evil and sin in the world and in our hearts were accepted as the primary sources of human suffering (we refer to it as pathology today), so biblical truth and spiritual battles for the heart were the solutions.

With the growing acceptance of so-called scientific explanations for human suffering (psychology and psychiatry), the 20th century brought with it alternative theories, most of which directly contradicted the biblical view of human suffering. David Powlison, in his work *Competent to Counsel*, reacts to the church's abdicating the responsibility for soul care in the modern era.

> The "therapeutic" was triumphant. Psychiatry and psychotherapy displaced the cure of souls, reifying the medical metaphor, and so ordaining "secular pastoral workers to take up the task." Emotional and behavioral ills of the soul that once registered dislocations in a moral agent's relationships to God and neighbor were re-envisioned as symptomatic of a patient's mental and emotional illness. Worry, grumbling, unbelief, lovelessness, strife, vicious habit, and deceit came to be seen though different eyes, as neurotic, anxiety, depression, inferiority complex, alienation, social maladjustment, addiction, and unconscious ego defense. Hospital, clinic, and office displaced church and community as the locus of cure.[5]

In the mid 1950s, evangelical Christians did not have educational programs to equip or train those entering ministry to engage in face-to-face care or healing of souls. Few Christian books dealt with the specific and prevalent common problems and the process of specific biblical change. Practical theology involved preaching, missions, evangelism, church government, and administration. Discipleship training consisted of doctrine, morals, and some life application skills, all of this much more focused on intellectual knowledge than on heart and life transformation. At that time in our history, there was no systematic analysis for care of the soul in the local church.

The 20th century brought with it the proliferation of the modern secular psychologies and the mental health industry. The church's authority as the primary institution for human sanctification began to diminish. Powlison again correctly noted the logical outcome: "Without a well-developed practical theology of change and counseling—and without the institutions, books, and practitioners to embody and communicate such—churchly resources were reduced to religious forms in abstraction from systematic understanding: a prayer, a Bible verse, a worship service, a banished demon, a creed, a testimony, an exhortation, a commitment. Should these fail, there were no options but referral out to the secular experts."[6]

> Direct and indirect support of the disciplines (not the terms) of psychology and psychiatry by the Christian community is an unspoken admission that the Word of God and the Spirit of God are insufficient resources to meet the deepest needs of man. The indictment here is not of the psychologist or the psychiatrist but, rather, of the institutions of theological training which have deferred to the developments of the world system and thereby turned out generations of ministers with an inferiority complex.
>
> —CHARLES R. SOLOMON, *Handbook for Christ-Centered Counseling*

Now we can clearly see that the Bible became less significant for objectively illuminating and addressing the human condition, pain, sin, and suffering. God became less relevant with regard to the human psyche because of the burgeoning scientific explanation for human suffering. The church bought into an unhealthy and seemingly uninformed dependence on secular soul-care practitioners. As we now know, the birth of these relatively new modernist disciplines offered only a superficial explanation for analysis and cure of the human soul. The practice of soul care began to be outsourced to professionals in the mental health field. Additionally, the concept of all believers as ministers in the church was relegated to a more professional model of the pastor and other ministers doing all or most of the pastoral care. The needs of the suffering saints far exceeded the ability and time of pastors to perform soul care.

While all of our experiences play an important and significant role in who we are, personal responsibility truly seems to be a thing of the past in our culture. Society began to change radically in the later part of the 20th century. Even in the Christian community we see a high divorce rate, sexual immorality, and acceptance of the therapeutic culture within churches across the nation. What are the specific implications for the Church of our Lord Jesus Christ?

"The rise of professionalism and secular psychologies in the 19th and 20th centuries effectively reduced the church's authority in this vital area of soul care. By the middle of the twentieth century, secular psychology and psychotherapy was firmly entrenched as the only legitimate approach to the study of human nature and to soul care. Rightly interpreted, modern soul care should be seen as the chief religious competitor to Christian salvation in the West."[7]

Early on Christians justified the use of professional psychotherapists based on a faulty view of mankind. The prevailing "trichotomist anthropology" based on two popular verses (1 Thess. 5:23 and Heb. 4:12) saw humankind as having three separate and distinct parts—spirit, soul, and body. Some took this view and developed a compartmentalized methodology for soul care. They wrongly assumed that we need a doctor to treat the body, a mental health professional to treat the soul (mind, emotion, and will), and a pastor to treat the spirit.

Most current Bible scholars would rightly argue that this approach was based on an incomplete "theoretical epistemology." Even current medical science disproves this error of compartmentalization, not from a biblical perspective but from an empirical one. It's conceptually naïve to treat any sphere of our being in isolation. An accurate biblical anthropology clearly demonstrates an "essential unity" among these three "parts" of human beings (Bible scholars indicate that the *Trinity* functions with an "essential unity" even though they may not use this specific term). We cannot separate body, soul, and spirit even though each has a distinct function according to God's plan and design.

## THROWING POSTMODERNISM INTO THE MIX

The logical outcome of individualism, rationalism, and existentialism are becoming even more apparent today in the aftermath of postmodernism: mankind's reason and experience defining "reality" and moral relativism is dominating our culture today. We also see the move toward greater levels of individualism, in direct contrast to the foundational element of community necessary for health in the body of Christ. The importance of relationships and community has been trumped by the "right" of self-expression and individual freedom, regardless of the impact our acts or attitudes may have on other people. Because we have lost our moral compass, our sense of right and wrong, it is now acceptable to project responsibility for our sins onto any number of objects, including the environment, our family, poverty, or other people.

Postmodernism in many respects is an attempt to correct some of the excesses and distortions of modernism. In a number of respects, change, embodied by the emerging church, is bringing some needed dialogue and change within the church. The movement often favors the use of simple story and narrative, even embracing mystery in order to reunify intellect and experience. Some would argue that this movement brings welcome authenticity and transparency into the church. Resurgence of the value of community and of good works or social activism as well as emphasis on missional living are welcome winds of change. Many in the emerging movement emphasize the here and now and the need to welcome the kingdom of heaven on earth, as opposed to primarily focusing on eternal life.

While rightly questioning some of the tenets that modernism held as dogma, postmodernism has swung to the opposite extreme from the scientific method into relativism and the rejection of absolute truth. As our culture has moved from modernism to postmodernism, truth based on the reason of mankind, observable phenomena, and the rights decried by certain communities or groups has been rejected for individualized truth structures. The result is lack of acceptance by many that a supreme truth even exists.

Psychological theory takes many forms in our postmodern, radically relative culture. Scores of theories attempt to explain the plight of mankind; few of them, however, agree philosophically on the nature of man. Current mental health statistics reveal that more people are diagnosed with mental health problems than ever before in our history. Presently, more mental health professionals are available to treat these maladies. We have more problems and more professionals but often without any standard for right and wrong, good and bad. So the central measure of anything then becomes self. Another concern is that unless the Bible is held firmly as our ultimate truth source, scriptural truth can be replaced with experience and mysticism. The comments about psychology are intended to be informative so that we will critically examine our theology of caring and align it with God's truth.

## IT'S TIME FOR A REVOLUTION

This is a pivotal time for the Church of our Lord Jesus Christ. We must engage the hurting, not automatically refer them. God has anointed the local church to reach into the hearts of hurting members and offer the community a message of hope and healing. Let's reach back into our rich history and learn from our fathers, borrow from science when it supports the truth of Scripture, and challenge a culture desperate for answers that only our Creator possesses. Let's take back the responsibility we forfeited and work together for the health and glory of His kingdom.

## NOTES

1. Eric. L. Johnson, *Foundations for Soul Care* (Downers Grove: InterVarsity Press, 2007), 53.
2. Thomas C. Oden, *Pastoral Counsel*, vol. 3 of *Classical Pastoral Care* (Grand Rapids: Baker, 1987), 58.
3. *www.britannica.com/EBchecked/topic/115240/Christianity/67548/History-of-Christian-mysticism*, accessed November 17, 2008.
4. Johnson, *Foundations for Soul Care*, 55.
5. David A. Powlison, "Competent to Counsel? The History of a Conservative Protestant Anti-Psychiatry Movement." Diss. Univ. of Pennsylvania, 1996, 41-42.
6 David A. Powlison, "Cure of Souls (and the Modern Psychotherapies)," *The Journal of Biblical Counseling*, spring 2007, 6.
7. Johnson, *Foundations for Soul Care*, 69.

# RECLAIMING

## *the*

# CHURCH'S

## CHARGE

It is good in mixed assemblies to mingle comfort that every soul may have its due portion. But if we have this for a foundation truth, that there is more mercy in Christ than sin in us, there can be no danger in thorough dealing.

—RICHARD SIBBES, *The Bruised Reed*

*Shepherd God's flock among you, not overseeing out of compulsion but freely, accordingly to God's will; not for the money but eagerly; not lording it over those entrusted to you, but being examples to the flock. And when the chief Shepherd appears, you will receive the unfading crown of glory.*

—1 PETER 5:2-4

# Genesis of the Christian Counseling Revolution

As you read this book, I hope you sense the need to reclaim the church's calling to care for the souls in our congregations and communities. Many providential elements are falling into place, and you can be part of the solution. In the past 50 years, a counseling revolution has occurred. Committed Christ followers have begun to counsel, research, and write about counseling; and we are now educating counselors in our seminaries and Christian universities.

The Christian Integration movement was developed in part by Clyde Narramore in the 1960s. Gary Collins carried this concept of integration forward as it grew in popularity. This movement is characterized by carefully integrating Christian theology with the theories, therapeutic methods, and professional roles of modern psychologies.

Another group developed from the passion and conviction of Jay Adams. This approach is best described as a commitment to the Bible alone (a non-Reformation view of *sola scriptura*) as the sole source of counsel. Many who hold to this view reject science, medication, or any inclusion of modern psychology in the counseling process.

In general, these two schools of thought on the Christian counseling—the Integration Model and the Nouthetic Model—are on opposite ends of the spectrum. While there are positive attributes to both, these models are most often viewed as polemical, so we should examine them for perspective.

The Integration Movement cannot yet precisely define itself. For many proponents and practitioners, modern psychology and the Bible are equally authoritative when diagnosing and treating human suffering. Careful evaluation leads one quickly to see a loose eclecticism associated with such an approach, even if well-meaning practitioners operate as if the Bible trumps psychology. An eclectic approach can be confusing to the recipient when the counselor borrows a bit from the Bible and a bit from a psychology based on modern and postmodern suppositions.

The Jay Adams, or Nouthetic approach (from the Greek word meaning "admonish or confront"), presents a different set of problems. Some followers of this methodology tout the sufficiency of Scripture and view psychology as heretical. Other Nouthetic counselors believe something can be learned from psychology. They have the view that Scripture can transform us but also understand that the Bible is not exhaustive. In other words they realize that God's truth cannot be effectively communicated in proof-texts to a soul in agony. While generalizations are dangerous, many professional Christian counselors view this model as insensitive and leaning toward a dangerous form of Biblicism.

## The Revolution Builds Momentum

The philosophy of soul care in the modern church usually falls somewhere between the Integrationist and the Nouthetic approach. We cannot accurately integrate or blend theology with secular psychologies based on humanistic philosophies. On the other hand, we should not wholly reject the psychological, especially that which aligns with biblical truth. This book's intent is not to engage in a study of the integration of theology and psychology or to go in the other extreme. Each church should conduct due diligence in selecting materials and leaders. Some materials maintain Scripture as foundational in their models (like the Picking Up the Pieces resources), while others may take liberties with texts and fit them to a therapeutic model.

Most pastors and conservative theologians realize psychological disciplines offer some necessary truths and some valid practice methodologies. They understand that though the Bible may not offer exhaustive information as a proof-text for counseling, it should never be subordinated to secular psychologies. All application of Scripture, including soul care, demands that we engage in a theological and interpretive task.

## New Research and Directions

We are seeing the development of sophisticated theological studies related to specific disorders of the soul. We are realizing that systematic theological study, from both analytical and larger story perspectives, must be incorporated into the discussion of Christian counseling. Seminaries and graduate programs are responding to this necessity; and in the future we'll see the development and refinement of biblical counseling programs for the pastor and professional practitioner. We are currently witnessing the emergence of a society dedicated to the advancement of a true Christian psychology for the professional.

Should we be concerned about those who engaged in formal psychological study initially without the benefit of formal theological training? It depends. Many evangelical leaders believe that psychological study submitted to critical biblical and theological scrutiny will lead to a true Christian psychology. By definition a biblical or Christian psychology will support the local church and direct the hurting to Christ and the church.

> *Jesus told him, "I am the way, the truth, and the life. No one comes to the Father except through me. If you know Me, you will also know My Father. From now on you do know Him and have seen Him."*
> —John 14:6-7

If truth is that which is ultimately, finally, and absolutely real, that truth is utterly trustworthy and dependable. Therefore, both accuracy and authenticity are important to truth. As Os Guinness says, "Belief in something doesn't make it true; only truth makes a belief true." If this is the case, then truth by definition is absolute.

The Christian faith is not true because it works; it works because it is true. It is not true because we experience it—we experience it deeply and gloriously—because it is true. It is not simply "true for us"; it is true for any who seek in order to find, because truth is true even if nobody believes it and falsehood is false even if everybody believes it.

—Os Guiness, *Time for Truth*

Today's prominent "self-psychology" encourages man to conform truth to his desires. A Christ follower, by definition, allows the Holy Spirit to transform his desires to correspond with truth. However, many Christians (as evidenced by the divorce rate and other cultural indicators) live according to the societal norm, not a biblical worldview. Many believe their faith is true because in some instances "it works" (pragmatism) because they feel "it is true according to their experience" (subjectivism) or because they believe it is "true for them and may not be true for others" (relativism).

God is both the author and sustainer of truth, and the Bible is our ultimate authoritative source. We must defend core truth against any philosophy, theory, or system that contradicts God's nature or the nature of man. While psychology can be helpful, it cannot change man's nature or his future. Only a persevering walk of faith in Jesus Christ can provide us with the abundant life we so desire.

The church is a community of Christ followers who should adhere to biblical principles, yet we (evangelicals included) are accepting and supporting philosophies that betray our convictions. As Christians we should require that Christian counseling be operationally defined and performed by practitioners who remain faithful to biblical authority. Otherwise we're not confronting this postmodern therapeutic culture; we're supporting it.

## Engaging the Secular Dialogue

Knowledge from sources other than the Bible is important in the area of caring for and healing souls. However, the mainstream mental health industry bases its "work" or product on symptom reduction and theories that don't acknowledge God, sin, or redemption. While there *is* a place for professional counseling, my primary concern is that the church has little or no influence on its members outsourced to professionals, has abdicated its role as the authoritative institution for soul care, and no longer provides places of ministry within the body for those God has gifted to minister to others.

Psychological research has great value. Neuropsychological assessment reveals much about brain structures and their function. Physiological psychology explains how stress and trauma affects physical health. However, studies based on a human view that is inconsistent with biblical truth will produce an invalid result and/or justify false beliefs and sin.

Christians should not fear secular education. Moses was well educated in Egypt (Acts 7:22). Daniel and his friends studied every branch of Chaldean literature (Dan. 1:17). Paul was a man of great learning (Acts 22:3; 26:24). Moses, Daniel, and Paul interpreted their learning through God's redemptive truth in order to achieve His purpose. Paul could quote an anthropologist who studied life in Crete (Titus 1:12), and he used the words of Greek philosophy in his argument in Athens (Acts17:28). Paul's familiarity with culture and knowledge from extrabiblical sources was invaluable during his missional ministry.

We could easily argue that our purpose should be the same as Paul's. Our mission field is a community of damaged souls whom God wishes to redeem and sanctify. These people (many of whom are lost) are searching for answers, and they're not particular where they find them. Families are fragmented, marriages are collapsing, and souls are aching to experience the love and acceptance of community. Their pain may drive them to a counselor who will help them feel better about their sin or to a counselor who will communicate our God's message of healing and redemption that is lived out in the local church.

## CHURCHES BEGINNING TO RESPOND

Many churches are developing biblical counseling ministries. In larger churches these ministries act as an extension of the pastor. Smaller churches often develop relationships with professional counselors in the community or congregation. Seminaries are beginning to take biblical counseling and soul care more seriously. However, we still need to engage professional Christian psychologists and counselors more enthusiastically if we hope to move the field away from secularism toward biblical truth.

Many churches are implementing small groups with a strategic purpose. These groups provide a valuable ministry by reaching into the congregation and reaching out to the community. Their purpose is to welcome people with specific needs—depression, divorce recovery, marital problems, addictions, and many others. Professional Christian counselors are learning that referring counselees to these groups expedites healing and improves treatment efficacy.

We should applaud the efforts of these churches for implementing some form of soul-care ministries and topic-specific groups intended to meet the hurting at their point of need. These groups provide a valuable function, teaching participants to confront pain and crises in a biblical fashion. They build a sense of trust, community, and interdependence. These dynamics are sorely lacking in many of our churches today. As long as the content of these groups is doctrinally sound and Christ honoring, members grow in their faith, their value to the kingdom, and their value to one another.

## Church Constraints

Most churches don't possess the institutional structures necessary to provide a full-orbed approach for soul care (discipleship, care for the hurting, and pastoral counseling). Those that do have the infrastructure may not be well structured to protect against an increasingly litigious culture. The local church is God ordained and should respond to the current fragmented approach to pastoral care with ecclesiastical oversight and implementation of structures for soul care. I agree with Dr. Powlison as he admonishes the church:

> The Bible ... addresses not only ideas and practices, but also social structure. Does the Holy Spirit intend that we develop a normative social institution for curing souls? The answer is yes. The church—as the Bible defines it—contains an exquisite blending of leadership roles and mutuality, of specialized roles and the general calling. It is the ideal and desirable institution to fix what ails us."[1]

Powlison clearly and accurately states that we can no longer allow our views on counseling to be matters of opinion and conscience. The Christian who counsels must view man as God does, he must counsel as God directs, and his primary focus must be identification with God's interests in the souls of people who are hurting. The church must address three general categories in order to bring about the realization and implementation of an effective soul-care ministry.

1. We must learn to apply and articulate biblical wisdom conceptually in soul-care efforts. We must be responsible to train those called into this ministry to use a biblical, relational model of evangelism, discipleship, and progressive sanctification.
2. We must apply biblical wisdom methodologically so that group or face-to-face soul care fits the Great Commission and the church's mission.
3. We must embody biblical wisdom in the church to produce an institutional structure that provides hope and healing for its members, especially those with limited financial means.

With the support and direction of Christian scholars and theologians, the church can confront our history of passivity. With God's help and direction, we can now begin the process of taking back what we relinquished to the world.

## A Fresh Movement Afoot

Christ followers and Christian organizations are mounting a charge to challenge the chaos of secular counseling and the secular mental health movement. Ministers and lay leaders must "choose this day whom you will serve" and pray for discernment. Certainly we will slip and fall along the way, but let's make sure we are moving in the right direction. Here is the reality: we must come to agree on the major issues and together get involved in a process of taking back that which we have forfeited.

Following is a limited list of organizations I've dealt with over time. Excellent Christ-centered research is ongoing in almost every area of life and suffering. I've provided a list of books on our Web site (*www.heartlifesoulcare.org*) with my disclaimer; we're adding to it all the time. The following list of organizations may prove helpful for smaller congregations looking for professional help or resources. Both AACC and Focus on the Family maintain an extensive list of Christ-centered professional counselors.

- HeartLife Professional Soul-Care resources page (*www.heartlifesoulcare.org*)
- LifeWay Christian Resources (*www.lifeway.com*)
- American Association of Christian Counselors—AACC (*www.aacc.net*)
- Christian Counseling and Educational Foundation (*www.ccef.org*)
- Focus on the Family (*www.focusonthefamily.com*)
- FamilyLife (*www.familylife.com*)
- Smart Marriages (*www.smartmarriages.com*)
- Faithful and True Ministries (*www.faithfulandtrueministries.com*)
- Institute for Sexual Wholeness (*www.sexualwholeness.com*)
- Restoring the Heart Ministries (*www.rthm.cc*)
- PeaceMaker Ministries (*www.peacemaker.net*)

## Join the Revolution

Our churches must lovingly challenge well-meaning, professional Christian counselors to explain their approaches. Good treatment follows good diagnosis. Whatever the cost we must advocate and support truth. A legitimate biblical or Christian psychology will defend God's truth against any philosophy, theory, or system that contradicts His nature or the nature of man.

Professionals operate primarily on a fee-for-service basis, so Christian professionals depend on the Christian community for referrals. It's prudent and necessary to understand a counselor's personal testimony, approach to counseling, and training. Some questions and background may be helpful. The local church is a primary market for professionals whose income depends on referrals. Churches have great influence over professional soul-care providers.

Churches must also get serious about soul care. Begin the journey and maintain ongoing emphasis on continuing to capture deepening levels of soul care in your church family.

NOTES

1. David Powlison, "Cure of Souls (and the Modern Psychotherapies)," *The Journal of Biblical Counseling*, spring 2007, 30.

# PICKING UP THE PIECES RESOURCES

## REAL HELP FOR REAL PEOPLE LIVING REAL LIFE.

How do we make sense of the times of pain and suffering in our lives? How can we reconcile the reality of our pain with the goodness of God?

Whenever you struggle, God's heart aches for you. He desperately wants to walk with you through the difficult and desperate times of your life so He can lead you to hope, healing, and freedom. Picking Up the Pieces is a series of honest, experiential Bible studies that will help you along the unfamiliar journey of rediscovering your heart!

- Written by leading therapists from the American Association of Christian Counselors
- Honest, experiential Bible studies that will set captives free from destructive patterns
- Probing questions for your heart and for God to help bind up the broken places
- Unique journaling experiences at the end of each session
- Replaces beauty for ashes and glory for shame

## GREAT RESOURCES FOR:

- Support Groups
- Small Groups
- Accountability Groups

- Recovery Groups
- Church Classes and Soul-Care Ministries
- Counseling Centers